IT MAY HARM YOUR DEFENCE

Alexander Hebdon

Published in 2024 by Patterdale Publishing

This work depicts actual events truthfully as the author's recollection
and extensive research permits. The author has made every effort to ensure
that the figures and information in this book were correct at the time of going
to press, and assumes no responsibility or liability for errors, inaccuracies,
omissions, or other inconsistencies.

ISBN 978-1-7385637-0-8
Also available as an ebook

Page design and typesetting by SilverWood Books
www.silverwoodbooks.co.uk

ALEX HEBDON lives near Hull and has always been fascinated by the law and the criminal justice system. He served in the Humberside Police for thirty years before retiring as a sergeant in 2017. He specialised in the video interviewing of children and other vulnerable victims and witnesses (including victims of domestic violence) and used his experience to train other officers.

During his service with the police, Alex was involved in several serious and complex investigations, and has given evidence in court on numerous occasions. He always wanted to observe a trial right the way through, something which was not possible as a police witness. Like a lot of people, he was intrigued by the archaic rituals and procedures of a crown court and was curious about their origins.

Having spent a third of his career working in the Goole area, Alex took a close interest in a murder case which happened in a quiet East Yorkshire village in the area he used to cover. It was such an unusual and interesting case that, having observed the whole trial at Hull Crown Court, he felt compelled to write this book.

In memory of Faye Wylie 1990-2024
A brave, intelligent and inspirational woman
who was taken too soon

Contents

THE STORY

1	Introduction	9
2	The Background to the Case	16
3	The Incident	21
4	The Trial	25
5	The Prosecution Case	31
6	The Offence of Murder	34
7	The Offence of Manslaughter	36
8	The Defence Counsel	38
9	The Witnesses	40
10	The Jury	46
11	The Principle of Open Justice	49
12	The Prosecution Evidence	52
13	The Caution	70
14	Adverse Inferences	75
15	The Reporters	78
16	The Case for the Defence	82
17	The Jury's Deliberations	94
18	The Retrial	103
19	The New Jury	107
20	The Prosecution Case II	110
21	Another Strange Turn of Events	114
22	Trial Number Three	118
23	The Evidence of the Forensic Pathologist	122
24	Catch-Up Day	128
25	The Completion of the Prosecution Case	134
26	The Case for the Defence II	140

27	The Judge's Directions	155
28	The Closing Speech of the Prosecution	157
29	The Closing Speech of the Defence	160
30	The Judge's Summing Up	162
31	The Verdict	168
32	The Sentencing Hearing	173

REFLECTIONS AND ANALYSIS

33	The Trial(s)	184
34	The Principle of Open Justice II	187
35	Domestic Abuse	194
36	Teresa Hanson's Evidence	198
37	What Really Happened?	208
38	A Reconstruction	212
39	The Future	216
Acknowledgements		219

1

Introduction

This is the true story of an extraordinary incident which occurred in a small village in East Yorkshire during the Christmas holiday of 2022. It was reported that a middle-aged grandfather had lost his life at his home in West Cowick and the police were investigating the circumstances. As a retired police sergeant who used to cover this area, I naturally took a keen interest in events as they unfolded. I was curious to find out what had happened in this quiet village near Goole. Eventually the police said that a fifty-three-year-old woman known to the victim had been arrested and they weren't looking for anyone else.

I followed this bizarre story on the television and in the newspapers as the details emerged. Paul Hanson, aged fifty-four, had been the victim of a fatal stabbing, and his wife of thirty-three years, Teresa Hanson, had been charged with his murder and was remanded in custody. Kingston-upon-Hull Magistrates' Court transferred the case to the Crown Court, where she appeared before Judge John Thackray on 3 January 2023. He set a trial date of 12 June 2023 and, surprisingly for a murder, granted her bail. What on earth had happened in this respectable family home? What were the events leading up to this dreadful incident? I was determined to find out.

This is the story of the trial – dramatic on some occasions, farcical on others. With the exception of the opening day of administrative procedures, I was present for every moment of the trial and listened to every piece of evidence. I was able to hear all the witnesses give their live testimony and the scientists give their expert opinions. I listened to the harrowing recordings of the 999 calls and watched the reactions of the defendant, her family and the jury. I followed the case right through to its dramatic conclusion.

Of course, it isn't possible to write down or recall everything, but what I have recorded in this book is taken either from my notes or from how I remember it. My memory isn't perfect, so minor details may be incorrect or inexact, but any such errors are trivial and do not impair the accuracy of the story I will tell; I have been careful to retain the essence of what was said and to preserve the meaning while remaining objective and impartial. I have occasionally offered an opinion or imagined what may have happened in certain instances, but I have made it clear where this is the case.

In the interests of balance and fairness, I have made three separate attempts to contact a representative of the family (through an intermediary) to offer them the opportunity to comment on what I have written and to give their own point of view. On the first request, I had no response from the intermediary. On the second and third attempts, I used a different intermediary and they confirmed they had passed on the request but had received no reply on each occasion.

What do you know about the law and the criminal justice system? Are you familiar with the court process and how a trial works?

Unless you work in the legal profession or have other relevant experience, your knowledge is probably restricted to what you see on television. This may come from crime dramas, which appear extremely exciting, with lots of twists and turns, ignoring all the tedious red tape and drudgery of real life. You might enjoy watching 'true life' crime documentaries consisting of numerous 'reconstructions' which need to be heavily edited in order to fit a one-hour slot, and which thus omit a lot of the details. These television shows are often about the crime itself, followed by the investigation. Rarely is any time given to the trial – the final chapter – other than a short scene or footnote informing viewers of the verdict and sentence. Occasionally you may see a film, television drama or play in which the trial is actually the central theme. For dramatic effect, these will often feature a clever barrister securing a conviction against all the odds, or an acquittal to prevent a miscarriage of justice. Out of nowhere and with incredible insight, they will land a 'knockout blow' by asking a key witness the crucial incisive question which undermines their testimony and brings their case down like a house of cards. This brings the trial to a juddering halt, with the rival barrister metaphorically waving a white flag and the victorious King's Counsel (KC) becoming the hero of the day. You won't be surprised to learn that trials are very rarely – if ever – like this.

Filming, recording and photography are forbidden in courts of law in England and Wales except on very rare occasions. Artists' impressions of, for example, the defendant or an expert witness cannot be drawn or painted contemporaneously; they are usually created later, from memory. The news broadcast will normally feature a reporter outside the court, relaying details of the latest piece of evidence given by the defendant or a crucial witness. Later, in a 'breaking news' story, the reporter will bring you the verdict of the jury, the defendant's reaction and the judge's final remarks. (Unfortunately, in the event of a guilty verdict the sentence is often deferred pending reports, which is a bit of an anticlimax.) On these occasions the court building may well form the backdrop to add to the drama, especially in a live broadcast. You will seldom see or hear a journalist reporting from the studio. This is not just for context but also because outside the court is the first place from which they can legally film in the race to break the news. If you look closely, you will notice that the reporter may be situated on the footpath or in another public area, and not immediately outside the court building itself.

This is because filming is prohibited not only inside the building but also within the 'precincts' of the court, which usually consist of a large 'apron' leading up to the steps or the main entrance.

The Criminal Justice Act 1925 (passed before the era of television) specifically forbids the taking of photographs or the drawing of sketches in "the precincts of the building". More recently, the Contempt of Court Act 1981 adds sound recording to the list of banned activities. You may think that this contributes to the mystique and intrigue of the court process, or you may think that a 'behind closed doors' culture exists and that members of the public are not welcome.

So why all the restrictions, when the principle of open justice has been widely accepted for centuries? We frequently hear the mantra that not only must justice be done, it must also be *seen* to be done. If the authorities are serious about open justice in this modern, technological age, why aren't there official live video streams of court proceedings? It should be a simple process to log on remotely and follow a trial. The technical facility already exists as a legacy from the Covid pandemic. Such recordings could be controlled internally and watched remotely. They could be made available at a later date, and even edited if necessary.

Journalists can and do watch remotely, and this, in theory, can also be done by a member of the public – at the judge's discretion. However, the application process is lengthy: you must justify your request, undertake not to record the footage, and answer numerous questions. It is, therefore, hardly surprising that this option is very rarely taken up. I get the impression that in reality it is only there for trusted journalists. The next best thing, you may think, would be to order a transcript of the case, which is sound-recorded as a matter of routine. This service has been privatised and is eye-wateringly expensive. At the time of writing, the company providing the service for the North-East region was called Opus. For Crown Court hearings it was 'price on application' but, as a guide, the cheapest rate quoted for hearings other than the Crown Court was £1.71 for every seventy-two words. Based on this, I estimate that a full transcript would have cost in excess of £1,000 per day.

I am sure that this is not an issue that troubles many ordinary people. After all, they can read about a trial in the newspaper. In the past, trials were reported on by local newspapers and regional television. But unfortunately, local newspapers are dying out, and regional television is going the same way, as the local stations pool their resources and technology. The result seems to be that only the trials that interest the public at a national level get widespread coverage, such as the so-called 'Wagatha Christie' case, even though that was a civil case of libel. Minor crimes that are only of local interest will be reported simply by naming the person, the crime of which they are convicted, and the sentence.

If you are interested in a specific case and wish to follow the trial in detail and experience the real-life drama and the very complicated legal processes, I'm afraid that, realistically, the only way to do that is to attend in person. This is exactly what I did, and even so, as I found, it is not as straightforward as you might imagine. I discovered that unless you are either a journalist or have a vested interest in the case (such as being family of the victim or the defendant), you are viewed with suspicion by all concerned – tolerated at best, but certainly not welcome. It is a massively time-consuming commitment in which there is a lot of hanging around and waiting, as nobody can predict what is going to happen next.

Lord John Atkinson, the judge in the 1912 case of *Scott v Scott*, said:

> *The hearing of a case in public may be, and often is, no doubt, painful, humiliating, or deterrent both to parties and witnesses...but all this is tolerated and endured, because it is felt that in public trial is to be found, on the whole, the best security for the pure, impartial and efficient*

With this in mind, I decided I would attend a full trial at Crown Court, observe the whole process and see for myself how 'open' justice actually is.

Attending a significant and high-profile case was something I had been planning for a long time. As a former police officer I have been a part of numerous Crown Court trials. My role normally consisted of giving evidence for the prosecution, being cross-examined by the defence counsel, and promptly returning to normal duty. I had never sat through a complete trial before. I had never witnessed the legal wrangling, the frustrating delays, the full court atmosphere, or the drama of the verdict being delivered. For once I wanted to take a comprehensive and objective view of proceedings rather than observing them through the narrow lens of an investigating police officer. I wanted to study the judge and the barristers at work, observe members of the jury and interpret their body language as the evidence unfolded, and share the public gallery with several family members and witness the ways in which they reacted to the various revelations. I had no idea what a gripping case it would turn out to be. My observations began as an academic exercise looking at the principle of open justice, but ended up as a study of a very real human tragedy.

The case I attended was a murder trial, and I had read about the incident in the newspapers and heard about it on the local television news: a respected fifty-three-year-old woman had been accused of stabbing her husband to death during the Christmas holiday in a quiet village in East Yorkshire. Straight away, I was curious about the events that had led to this bizarre incident. Even for somebody with previous experience, what I witnessed was so fascinating that I began taking notes and, as events unfolded, decided to write this book. What follows is a commentary on the whole case, covering events both inside and outside the courtroom and the devastating impact on the family. It includes analysis of the tactics used by both the prosecution and defence counsels, with my own interpretation of the evidence and some legal explanation. I believe I was the only impartial observer to hear every piece of evidence.

2

The Background to the Case

Paul and Teresa Hanson had been together for thirty-seven years and married for thirty-three. They first met on a bus in 1985, when Paul was seventeen and Teresa was sixteen. They were travelling from their homes near Goole in East Yorkshire, and were on their way to college in Scunthorpe, North Lincolnshire. They struck up a conversation, saw each other regularly, and soon began dating. Four years later, in July 1989, they were married at the ages of twenty-one and twenty, and set up home in the village of Rawcliffe, near Goole. Paul worked in the construction industry and Teresa made her living as a hairdresser. They went on to have two children, Ryan (born 1991) and Sherri (born 1994), and had three grandsons, aged eight, five and two at the time of the alleged murder. By all accounts, Paul and Teresa were a close and loving couple with a very happy marriage. Ryan and Sherri had an idyllic childhood and upbringing, with Paul even building them a swimming pool in their back garden. The Hansons lived close to most of their extended family, whom they saw regularly.

Eventually the children grew up and left home, and in May 2017 Paul and Teresa downsized and moved to 21 Little London Lane in the nearby village of West Cowick. Neighbours described them as "a really lovely family". Number 21 is a modest two-bedroomed semi-detached 1950s house at the end of a row of properties; it has cream-coloured rendering, and open land to the rear and side. The house and garden both appear to have been extended. Paul and Teresa were now grandparents, who took an active role in helping to look after their grandchildren, with Teresa regularly doing the school run. Evidence of their grandchildren's regular visits could be seen in the back garden, which contained a football goal, a large trampoline, and children's toys. Also on show were indications of how they liked to spend their leisure time: a large hot tub underneath a wooden gazebo, and a separate barbecue area, both of which were said to be used regularly all year round. Parked on their drive would be Paul's white work van and Teresa's ten-year-old purple Volkswagen Golf convertible. Quite often their son's or daughter's car would be parked on the street as they picked up or dropped off their own children.

As a middle-aged couple, Paul and Teresa were able to enjoy their new-found freedom, and they had a very active social life. They were well known in the village and were frequently seen walking their dog, Kiki. Teresa had her own successful business, Little London Luxury's (sic), making and selling scented wax candles and melts. Paul was a construction site manager, which entailed very hard physical work. He enjoyed gardening, and spent a lot of his leisure time in the back garden. The couple spent time relaxing together in their hot tub with a bottle of red wine or enjoying a barbecue with the wider family. In the words of their son, Ryan, they had a "work hard, play hard attitude". They were at the stage where they could enjoy a few of the good things in life, such as exotic holidays and prestige cars. During the 2022 Christmas break, they booked a summer holiday to Cape Verde and also ordered a new car, which was due to be delivered in March 2023.

Paul had had a difficult upbringing after his father died when Paul was very young. His mother remarried, but Paul and his stepfather had a difficult relationship. His mother sided with her new husband, and Paul's relationship with her broke down.

A testing time in the Hansons' marriage came when Paul was involved in a serious road accident in March 1997 while travelling as a passenger in a car in thick fog on the M42 motorway. He sustained numerous serious injuries and eventually had to have his spleen removed. He was a patient in a Birmingham hospital for several weeks, and Teresa gave up work and moved into nurses' accommodation at the hospital to help take care of Paul until he was discharged. Their children were still very young, and the extended family rallied round to help look after them. Paul spent several months recovering at home and being cared for by Teresa, and eventually he had a phased return to work. This must have been a difficult time for the couple in terms of both their relationship and their financial situation.

In 2010 Paul was the victim of an unprovoked assault in a pub in the nearby town of Snaith. He sustained a serious head injury, which required brain surgery and another long lay-off from his job. Teresa again helped to nurse him back to health until he was fit to return to work. The head injury changed Paul's personality. According to Teresa, he became short-tempered and drank more. Alcohol also affected him more severely, and after a hard day's work he would return home and immediately start drinking, regularly falling asleep on the sofa by 8pm. These changes altered the dynamics of the relationship, and Teresa needed to be understanding and tolerant of his behaviour. They had occasional rows, which were often related to Paul's drinking. These usually involved shouting and the slamming of doors, as overheard by their neighbours in the adjoining house. Although the couple's arguments could be loud and aggressive, there was no known history of violence between them.

Christmas Day 2022 was a joyous occasion. The Hansons' home was adorned with numerous colourful decorations and had two large Christmas trees on display. Their two children and three grandchildren were present, as were Teresa's parents. They all wore party hats and enjoyed a traditional Christmas dinner in a crowded

Teresa and Paul Hanson on their
wedding day in July 1989

… and a few years before the
incident

Paul and Teresa enjoying time
in their hot-tub

… and on holiday

(Images courtesy of Enterprise News & Pictures)

and bustling dining room full of laughter and cheer. It was a typical scene, replicated across the country. Their daughter, Sherri, posted on Facebook: "We've had the best day today with family."

In the days following Christmas Day, Paul and Teresa took advantage of their time off to go shopping, walk the dog and visit relatives. They were looking forward to their holiday and were excited about their new car being delivered. They'd had a lovely Christmas, with time to relax and enjoy quality time with their loved ones. Everything seemed perfect. They were full of optimism and were preparing to welcome in the New Year and celebrate Teresa's fifty-fourth birthday on New Year's Day. Nobody could have imagined that by then Paul would be dead and Teresa would spend her birthday in prison.

On Wednesday 28 December, Paul and Teresa walked their dog, Kiki, visited Teresa's sister-in-law, and then went to the Tesco supermarket in Goole to get something for their evening meal. After a busy and tiring few days, they were looking forward to a quiet night in, having a meal and a drink, and enjoying each other's company. They returned home in the late afternoon, opened a bottle of Rioja, played some music, and even had a dance together. They had each drunk two or three glasses of wine by the time Teresa began preparing the evening meal of Mediterranean tart. Paul was in the living room, watching television.

What happened next would change their lives forever and devastate their family. It sent shock waves right through the local community, and led to the trial I observed.

3

The Incident

At 7.05pm on Wednesday 28 December 2022, a 999 call was made by Teresa Hanson and, at her request, was put through to the ambulance service. Despite it being an emergency call, it took one and a half minutes for an ambulance call taker to answer it. Teresa was in a distressed state and told the operator, "We had an argument and I stabbed him." The call lasted six minutes and forty-eight seconds, and set in motion a series of events.

The ambulance crew attended the address at 7.20pm and paramedics immediately began cardiopulmonary resuscitation (CPR) on Paul, who was lying in a pool of blood in the dining room – the same room in which the Hansons had enjoyed their Christmas dinner together only three days earlier. The police attended at 7.33pm, and at 7.35pm Teresa was arrested for assault with intent to cause grievous bodily harm, and was taken to Clough Road Police Station in Hull. At 7.50pm Paul was transported by ambulance to Hull Royal Infirmary, with the paramedics still working on him when he arrived at the casualty department at 8.20pm. He was immediately examined by the consultant, who found that there was no heartbeat and no cardiac electrical activity and so further attempts at resuscitation would be futile. He declared life extinct: Paul was dead. This news was relayed to the police at Clough Road, where Teresa was in custody, and at 9.02pm she was further arrested for the murder of her husband.

Over the next two days, Teresa was interviewed on three separate occasions, and after consultation with the Crown Prosecution Service (CPS) the police charged her with Paul's murder. She appeared at Kingston-upon-Hull Magistrates' Court on Saturday 31 December (the day before her fifty-fourth birthday), and was remanded in custody to appear before Kingston-upon-Hull Crown Court on Tuesday 3 January 2023. There, unusually for somebody facing a charge of murder, she was granted bail, on condition that she live at her parents' house in the nearby village of Rawcliffe Bridge, observe a curfew, give up her passport, and not discuss the case. She was seen to blow a kiss to members of her family in the public gallery. At a later hearing she pleaded not guilty and the trial was set to begin on 12 June 2023 and was expected to last five days.

The case was covered widely in local and national newspapers and featured heavily in local television news programmes. I can't remember exactly where I first read or heard about it, but it immediately caught my attention and interest, as I knew West Cowick quite well, having worked as a police officer in that area. I didn't know any of the family, as some years had passed since I had retired from the police, but I knew that West Cowick is a small, quiet village where crime of any sort is a rarity. Murder or manslaughter of a domestic nature is extremely rare in England and Wales. In the year ending March 2023, there were exactly 100 domestic homicides of which thirty of the victims were male (Office for National Statistics). Paul Hanson was one of them. Homicide offences don't normally involve respectable, hard-working couples with no history of offending or violence. I found myself reading as much as I could about the circumstances of the alleged crime, and was curious to know about the sequence of events leading up to this terrible tragedy.

When the time came, I had no commitments, so out of pure curiosity I decided I would attend the trial. Often, murder trials can

(Above) Police in attendance at 21 Little London Lane, West Cowick

(Below) Police guarding the scene with a Christmas tree and wreath still decorating the entrance   (Images courtesy of Richard Addison)

go on for weeks. Because there were no direct witnesses and much of the evidence was agreed between the prosecution and the defence, very few witnesses would be required to give their testimony on oath. As the trial was scheduled for only five days, I thought I could attend and hear all the evidence. I was interested not only in the trial itself but also in the workings of the court, with all its archaic traditions and rituals.

Crime Scene Investigators prepare to enter the house
(Courtesy of Richard Addison)

4

The Trial

The trial began as scheduled on Monday 12 June 2023 at Hull Crown Court. The court is a relatively modern building, having been completed in 1991 at a cost of £11.3 million, and stands on the corner of Alfred Gelder Street and Lowgate in Hull's Old Town district. It is a grand, imposing red-brick building, with a silver-domed circular atrium, a turret, a flagpole, and a coat of arms adorning the front of the building. At the entrance there is a large apron of open paving leading up to a broad set of seven steps which narrow as you approach the main doors. I don't know if the architects of court buildings have a brief to design them to inflict maximum intimidation upon first-time attendees, but if they do, they will certainly have earned their bonus for the design of Hull Crown Court.

The criminal courts are situated on the first floor and are reached by climbing a wide spiral staircase in the centre of the building. This leads to a large, circular concourse, with several rows of seats radiating out like the spokes of a wheel from the central staircase towards the offices on the periphery. Around the edge of the building there are six criminal courts, separated by corridors which lead to offices for barristers, police, the Witness Service, and other court workers. Defendants on bail, prosecution and defence witnesses, journalists, family members and humble observers such as myself all have to share the public space and be very careful what they say and to whom. During my 'stay' I became familiar not only with the various characters who work at the courts but also with the toilets, the vending machine, the water fountain and the coffee dispenser.

I was unable to attend on the first day, but I understand that proceedings started late and the day was taken up by legal discussions, the swearing in of the jury, and the indictment being formally read out. The next day, Tuesday 13 June, having struggled to find suitable parking, I eventually arrived at the main entrance at about 9.40am, not really knowing what to expect. For some reason courts don't begin work until 10am, and then the first half-hour is often taken up with bail hearings, warrant applications and other urgent business. I don't know why the court starts so late, but I presume it is to allow time for the solicitors, barristers and judges to prepare for the day's business, some of which they have to deal with at very short notice.

It was fortunate that I arrived early, because once you enter the building you have to join a long queue to go through an airport-style security check, which involves emptying your bag and pockets, removing your belt, watch and jewellery, walking through a metal-detecting arch, and being scanned by a security official with a wand. I fully understand why this is necessary, but it is a bind to go through it twice a day. Astonishingly, you have to wait in the queue with witnesses and even jury members, who can all take a close look at your personal belongings. Over time the security guards must have got used to me, but with one exception my cheery greetings were met with silence. You quickly learn to wear and carry the bare minimum.

Once I had got dressed again and climbed the stairs, I had to discover which court was hosting the trial. There was no obvious way to quickly find out, but outside each court is a monitor which has details of the scheduled cases on a loop system, with each page displayed for about five seconds. Blink and you miss it. After observing for three repeats of the loop, I discovered that the murder trial involving Teresa Hanson was being held in Court One and would get under way after the bail applications and other administrative business of the day. I sat on one of the many available seats and waited. Looking around, I observed the hustle and bustle of barristers in their wigs and gowns, scurrying to and from their offices and liaising with their clients on the public concourse. It was extremely busy, and I was trying to work out who everybody was: witnesses, family, defendants? Defendants in Crown Court trials are often in custody, but those who aren't share the same public area as a witness who may be about to give evidence against them.

Suddenly, an usher appeared outside Court One and said in a booming voice: "The case of Teresa Hanson."

I got up and politely allowed everybody else heading for Court One to go in front of me. This also allowed me to try to weigh up who the interested parties were. You don't get long to find a seat, and you are expected to somehow know where to go. I quickly worked out that there was a section for the police and other officials, a row of seats with a desk in front earmarked for the press, and the public gallery for everybody else. I think there were only two reporters, and the rest of the attendees took their seats in the public gallery. Most of the seats were quickly taken by people who I assumed were family members. The only seats remaining were in the front two rows. I thought I would be discreet and leave some space by sitting in the very front row.

Teresa was already in the dock – an area which stretches across the back of the room and, Hull being a modern court, is partitioned off with a glass screen for security reasons. Of course, Teresa was on bail and therefore unlikely to attempt an escape, but she was nevertheless accompanied by a court official. She would arrive every day along with the rest of her family, because one of the conditions attached to her bail was that she reside with her parents in the village of Rawcliffe Bridge, near Goole, some thirty miles and an hour's travelling each day. The judge had instructed her to arrive half an hour early and to remain for half an hour after the official adjournment of proceedings, in order to avoid interaction of any sort with the witnesses and the jury. Teresa and her family numbered about seven or eight in total, and they would take up a couple of rows of seats on the concourse each day and talk among themselves until she was required to take her place in the dock. It did seem strange that she could mingle with members of the public and wander into the city centre at lunchtime in between being tried for murder. Her face was familiar from the many photographs that had appeared in the newspapers and online. She is of small stature and stout build, with shoulder-length, greying dark brown hair which was sometimes tied back, and on the first day of her trial she was wearing a black top and black trousers. She wore this attire most days, and I am not sure if it was the type of outfit she would normally wear. Maybe she chose the outfit on the advice of her legal team, or perhaps it was an indication that she was still mourning the death of her husband.

Once everyone had settled into their seats, the clerk issued the instruction to "all rise" as the presiding judge entered the courtroom to take up his position on the bench, high above the rest of the court, with a commanding view of proceedings.

If you had never visited a court before, after watching the many formal rituals you could be forgiven for thinking that you had travelled back in time a few hundred years. Courts are steeped in history and tradition. Why do the judge and the barristers wear robes and wigs, for instance? It actually dates back to the fourteenth century, when robes would have been considered normal attire. The wearing of wigs became de rigueur during the seventeenth century when Charles II was on the throne, and went out of fashion in the 1800s during the reign of George III. It just seems that while the rest of society moved with the times, the courts were reluctant to do likewise. The term 'court' in its legal sense originates from the royal court, which is why every court in the land is adorned with the royal coat of arms and the senior court is known as the Crown Court.

Lawyers and court officials bow to the judge on entering because the judge is representing the reigning monarch. Technically, they are bowing not to the judge but to the King.

Please note: the judge in an English or Welsh court does not possess a gavel, and never has done. This common myth can only have come from television adverts or American dramas, in which the lawyers' every other word seems to be "Objection!" This is never said by barristers in our courts.

The judge in this case was Judge John Thackray KC, aged fifty-three and originally from Wakefield, who'd been a practising barrister for more than twenty-five years and a circuit judge for four. A circuit judge is a second-level judge, one step up from a recorder. In order to qualify as a circuit judge, you must have been a barrister for at least seven years or have previously been a recorder. Dressed in his finery of the traditional wig and gown, Judge Thackray looked young compared to the stereotypical Crown Court judge, and had a remarkable resemblance to Detective Chief Inspector (DCI) Frank Burnside (played by Christopher Ellison) from the television series *The Bill*.

Once everybody in the court had taken their seats, a short discussion about the schedule took place between Judge Thackray and the two barristers. The judge explained that they were "one judge down" this week and he was having to cover for a colleague, so things might have to be rearranged. The jury, who had been sworn in the previous day, were then shown into the court and took their allocated places on the jurors' bench. There were seven women and five men, who, understandably, looked very apprehensive and even uncomfortable with the strange surroundings and the huge responsibility that had been bestowed upon them.

Proceedings began with the outlining of the case by the prosecuting counsel, Alistair MacDonald KC. Aged sixty-nine, of stocky build and a ruddy complexion, he was well spoken with a southern accent. Dressed in the obligatory robe and wig, Mr

MacDonald had the appearance and demeanour of a barrister from *Rumpole of the Bailey*. He had been a barrister for forty years and a KC since taking silk in 2000. He was the chairman of the Bar Council in 2015, and belonged to New Park Court Chambers in Leeds.

5

The Prosecution Case

Alistair MacDonald summarised the prosecution case by describing the events of Wednesday 28 December 2022. The ambulance service received a telephone call from Teresa Hanson at 7.05pm stating that she had stabbed her husband "just out of anger…about five minutes ago". After giving further details to the ambulance call taker, the call dropped out, so she redialled 999 but was put through to the police. Recordings of both of these calls formed part of the prosecution evidence.

The ambulance crew arrived at 7.20pm and immediately began working on Paul before taking him to Hull Royal Infirmary. There was nobody else in the house other than Kiki the dog. The police arrived at the address at 7.33pm, and at 7.35pm they arrested Teresa for assault with intent to cause grievous bodily harm. Immediately before she was arrested, she made what is known as a 'significant statement' by saying to the arresting officer, "I didn't mean to do it. It was just an argument – I was making fucking tea." (A 'significant statement' is one which is unsolicited and can therefore be used in evidence even if the suspect hasn't been cautioned.) When the police arrived, there was a pan of caramelised onions on the hob, cooked, with the hob turned off.

At the hospital, Paul was declared dead at 8.24pm. Teresa was on her way to the police station in Clough Road in Hull, arriving at 8.57pm. At 9.02pm she was informed of Paul's death and was

Teresa Hanson leaving court accompanied by her daughter Sherri
(Alamy Stock Photo)

arrested for the offence of murder. The following day she consulted with, and was advised by, an accredited legal representative (not a qualified solicitor), who was present for all three interviews. Teresa, on the advice of her legal representative, gave the police a prepared statement to the effect that Paul had been verbally and mentally abusive to her over the years and that the injury had occurred after he had walked towards her while she was holding the knife. She then responded with "no comment" to all police questions in that interview and all subsequent interviews.

We were told that we would hear expert evidence from a forensic pathologist, who would confirm that the cause of death was a single stab wound to the chest, and that the chances of this occurring by accident were "highly unlikely". We would also hear from a forensic scientist, who would confirm that a kitchen knife with a four-inch blade had DNA on it matching that of Paul Hanson and was the likely murder weapon.

6

The Offence of Murder

Teresa was on trial for murder. There are many misconceptions about this offence, possibly because it is a common law offence. In other words, it is a historical crime which has evolved over the centuries, as opposed to statutory law, which is an act passed in Parliament and which carries with it a clear definition.

If you are not familiar with criminal law, your perception of murder might be that it requires 'malice aforethought', 'premeditation' or an 'intention to kill'. You are likely to have picked up these ideas from watching old murder mysteries on the television. You would be partially correct. The seventeenth-century judge Sir Edward Coke provided the earliest definition, which was first published in 1797 and states:

> *When a person of sound mind and discretion, unlawfully killeth any reasonable creature in being, and under the King's peace, with malice aforethought either express or implied.*

This definition still forms the basis of the current law in which, through adaptations for a modern world, case law and the use of contemporary language, murder is now accepted as meaning:

When a person of sound mind unlawfully kills another person and they have the intention to kill or to cause grievous bodily harm.

It has been held that 'malice aforethought' doesn't require planning or premeditation of the killing but just the required intention, even if that intention is formed immediately before the act. The intention need not be to actually kill the victim, as an intention to cause grievous bodily harm is sufficient. The term 'grievous bodily harm' itself is derived from the Offences Against the Person Act 1861, and has been held to mean 'really serious bodily harm'.

In all crimes, two elements must be present: mens rea (guilty mind) and actus reus (guilty act). For murder, the mens rea is to have the intention to kill or to do really serious harm and the actus reus is the act itself which causes the death. So the two common myths – that a murder needs to be premeditated and that the perpetrator must intend to kill their victim – are simply not true.

In order to convict Teresa of murder, the prosecution had to prove to the jury, beyond reasonable doubt, that she was responsible for the act that had caused the death of her husband and that she had intended to at least cause him really serious harm. The judge instructs the jury that they must be satisfied that they are sure before finding a defendant guilty. The burden of proof, or the onus, sits with the prosecution. It is not for the defence to prove the defendant's innocence.

7

The Offence of Manslaughter

Manslaughter is also a common law offence and, in accordance with Section 6 of the Criminal Law Act 1967, is an alternative verdict for the jury to consider if they don't believe that all the elements are present to convict for murder. As with murder, there must have been a deliberate act which caused the death of another, but if the jury believe that the defendant didn't have the necessary intent to cause at least serious bodily harm, they may find them guilty of manslaughter instead of murder. A common example we frequently hear about is the so-called 'one-punch manslaughter'. This normally involves an assault such as a punch to the face, following which the victim falls, bangs his head on the edge of a kerb, and later dies. Clearly the punch was a deliberate act, but the defendant will argue, with some justification, that although he intended to harm the victim, he neither intended nor foresaw the consequences of that single punch.

In this particular case, the problem for the defence team was that a conviction for manslaughter would be very difficult to justify, for two reasons. First, if Teresa maintained her claim that what had happened had been a terrible accident, then there was no deliberate act. Second, if she did admit that it was a deliberate act, it would be very difficult to argue that, in delivering a stab to the chest, she didn't intend or foresee really serious harm. If she was going to give evidence that the stabbing was unintentional, she was effectively 'rolling the dice'. It was going to be all or nothing. She must have been hoping that the jury would believe her evidence, in which case she couldn't be found guilty of anything – not even assault. If there was no criminal act and it was just an unfortunate accident, she would walk free. However, if the jury didn't believe her evidence, it would be very difficult to come to a 'compromise' verdict of manslaughter, because there would be no justification in law. The only option open to them in these circumstances would be to find her guilty of murder, which comes with a mandatory life sentence.

I think this was the dilemma of which everybody was aware. I don't believe there was a single person in the courtroom who thought she deserved to be imprisoned for life. Although manslaughter has a maximum penalty of life imprisonment, this is very rarely imposed, and the judge has wide discretion when it comes to sentencing for manslaughter. Teresa could, of course, have pleaded guilty to murder; but with only a slightly reduced minimum term of imprisonment in return for a guilty plea, there perhaps wasn't the incentive to do so.

8

The Defence Counsel

The barrister advising Teresa and tasked with sorting out this legal conundrum was Jason Pitter KC. Mr Pitter is certainly not your stereotypical barrister. A tall, slim, shaven-headed fifty-one-year-old former basketball player from the Chapeltown area of Leeds, he speaks with a strong northern accent, has been practising law since 1996, and in 2014 was the first black barrister on the northern circuit to become a QC (now KC). It made me wonder if somebody who was bald and normally wore a toupee would replace it with the formal wig each time they were in court, or whether they would put it on top and wear two wigs? Mr Pitter didn't wear a toupee, incidentally. He seemed very polite and down to earth, and always acknowledged me when I yielded to him or held the door when going into court. Perhaps he could have had a word with the security staff for me.

Interestingly, like Alistair MacDonald, Mr Pitter belonged to the New Park Court Chambers in Leeds. You would think that this would raise a few ethical questions about conflict of interest, but apparently it is common practice. Although it is illegal in some other countries (for example Germany), in this country barristers work independently, and chambers are not their employers or a partnership of barristers but merely a means of sharing the expense of offices, IT systems and staff. It still seems a bit inappropriate to me. It would be naive to think that barristers who work out of the same office, use the same IT system and employ the same staff would not be familiar with each other. Mr MacDonald was commissioned on behalf of the CPS because in a murder trial it is normal practice to appoint a KC as the prosecuting counsel. Mr Pitter was acting on behalf of the defence, possibly funded by legal aid.

At the time of writing, to qualify for legal aid at a Crown Court trial, your total household disposable income must be less than £37,500. However, if you are self-funding and are found not guilty, you are entitled to your money back plus interest. But as to how both barristers were appointed from the same chambers, and whether it was done deliberately for convenience or a matter of pure coincidence, I do not know.

9

The Witnesses

It is the responsibility of the prosecution to prove that the defendant is guilty of the offence for which they have been indicted. Even if certain facts seem obvious, all the necessary details must be given in evidence and must stand up to the scrutiny of cross-examination. To convict for murder, there must be evidence to prove:

1. A death has occurred.
2. The cause of death.
3. The defendant was responsible for the action which caused the death.
4. The action was deliberate.
5. The defendant intended to cause at least really serious harm to the victim.
6. There was no lawful justification, e.g. self-defence or an act of war.

In this particular case, there was no dispute about points 1, 2, 3 or 6, even though the evidence still had to be presented formally. The trial was really all about points 4 and 5. The defence accepted that Teresa was responsible for the act which had ended her husband's life, but claimed that the stabbing was not deliberate but was an unfortunate accident, and that therefore she did not intend to cause him *any* harm, let alone really serious harm. It wasn't a case of 'whodunnit' but rather 'howdunnit'.

The evidence to prove these points can take many forms, but is usually given or explained by somebody giving a verbal account under oath or affirmation from the witness box. They can be expert witnesses, who are specialists in their field and can therefore offer an expert opinion. Alternatively, they can be direct witnesses, who can give evidence of what they saw, heard, touched, smelled or tasted, or who can testify as to the defendant's character. Evidence can also take the form of physical objects or documents, which are presented to the court by the person who seized or created them. Examples might include the weapon used, the victim's clothing, 999 call recordings, CCTV footage, transcripts of police interviews, and photographs of the scene.

The job of the defence is to create sufficient doubt in the minds of the jury to make them unsure, or at least not sure enough to find the defendant guilty. They will frequently pick on the most vulnerable piece of evidence in the prosecution case in the hope that at least one of the points listed above is not proven sufficiently to persuade a jury to convict. Just a small gap in the evidence or a single unconvincing witness is all it takes for the prosecution to fail, because their case is only ever as strong as its weakest link.

The case was scheduled for five days, which seems quite a short period of time to try somebody for a crime as serious as murder. The reason for this, apparently, was because so much of the evidence was 'agreed' between the prosecution and defence. This means that written statements served prior to the trial would not be contested by the defence, because their content was accepted as true. There was no need, therefore, to require these witnesses to give evidence in person or to have that evidence tested by means of cross-examination. Instead, the majority of witnesses had their written statements read out to the jury. The knife used in this incident wasn't brought into the court, partly because there was no dispute about it being the object used to stab Paul, and partly to avoid causing unnecessary upset. For the same reason, no photographs of the victim were shown to the jury. Instead, diagrams and 'body maps' were used to explain the nature and location of any injuries. 'Evidence packs' containing numerous photographs, diagrams and transcripts were available to the jury, but not to the press or observers such as myself.

I am sure that it is common practice not to require witnesses to attend, as it saves time and money, and it may seem pointless to compel them to attend. However, I can't help feeling that a written statement read out by a barrister does not have nearly the same impact as somebody giving evidence in person. There is no emotion, no body language, and no opportunity to expand on what the witness originally said in their statement, which may have been made several months earlier. The statement is only as good as the police officer taking it at the time. This seems a poor substitute for the alternative of an experienced barrister, with all the information at their fingertips, taking the witness through their evidence. Is this compromise the best way to establish the truth, or merely a convenient method of saving time and money? I'm not sure.

There were ten witnesses for the prosecution but, incredibly, only three gave evidence in person. They were:

- Dr Michael Parsons (forensic pathologist and expert witness)
- Ryan Hanson (son of the defendant and the victim)
- Detective Constable (DC) Stuart Quinn (the police officer dealing with the case).

The remaining seven witnesses, whose evidence was accepted, had their witness statements read out by the prosecuting barrister, Alistair MacDonald. They were:

- Rachel Trafford (next-door neighbour)

- Shaun Trafford (next-door neighbour)
- Michelle Harvey (Teresa's sister-in-law)
- Andrew Hyland (paramedic)
- Police Constable Adam Lazenby (arresting police officer)
- Dr Paul Stewart (casualty doctor)
- Kathryn Bird (forensic scientist and expert witness).

Of the seven witnesses giving evidence for the defence, again, only three appeared in the witness box. They were:

- Teresa Hanson (defendant)
- Sherri Hanson (daughter of the defendant and the victim)
- Vanessa Lappin (sister of Paul Hanson).

The other four, who were all character witnesses, were friends and relatives of the defendant.

If a defendant is of bad character, only in rare circumstances can this be introduced as evidence by the prosecution. If, for example, the defence calls a witness who gives evidence of the accused's honesty in a theft trial, this opens the door for the prosecution to disprove this by listing their previous convictions for theft and fraud and suggesting to the jury that the defendant has a propensity to commit this type of crime. Of course, introducing such evidence is therefore a huge 'own goal' on the part of the defence, which is why a defendant with previous convictions will never introduce the subject of character.

Teresa was deemed to be of 'absolute good character', which means that she had no previous convictions of any kind and there was no evidence in her past of 'reprehensible behaviour'. Other than Teresa herself, the defence relied entirely on witnesses who gave evidence of her good character. So, in the murder trial in which

Teresa faced a possible life sentence, a total of six witnesses gave evidence in person, and if you discount family members (who were mostly character witnesses) you are left with:

- a forensic pathologist
- a police officer
- the defendant.

Court One is modern-looking, covered in light oak panelling, with the public gallery at the extreme left of the room with seven tiered rows of four cinema-style blue cloth seats, all facing the front of the court. Directly in front of the public gallery is a smaller area for police and court officials, looking side-on across the court. Ahead of the officials' seating area is the witness box, which is in front and slightly to the right of the public gallery. The desk and chairs allocated for members of the press are immediately adjacent to the public gallery to the right, but facing the court side-on and separated from the public by a wooden partition. At the opposite side of the court is the area occupied by the jurors, which consists of two rows of six seats looking across the room. It is reached via a separate entrance leading from the jury room, where they hold their private deliberations. The judge sits in an elevated position at the front of the court, reaching it from his official quarters (or 'chambers') via a private doorway. The clerk and the usher have seats immediately in front of the judge, but at floor level. Facing the judge, in the 'well' of the court and occupying the central area of the room, are the prosecution and defence teams, with the defence nearest the jury and the prosecution nearest the public gallery.

If you imagine the court as a football pitch, all the 'spectators' occupy seats around the perimeter of the stadium, facing inwards to get the best view of the action – with the exception of those in the public gallery. Family members, neutral observers and even witnesses are made to sit side-on and crane their necks to watch proceedings. I'm sure that this is not an accident but is designed to prevent members of the public eyeballing the jury and/or the witnesses giving evidence. The fact that there is a smoked-glass screen on top of the wooden partition through which you have to observe reinforces that view.

10

The Jury

If there was still any doubt about the rationale behind the seating arrangements for the public gallery, it very quickly disappeared during the first break in proceedings. As I mentioned, I was sitting in the very first line of seats to the extreme right of the public gallery; the family had all sat together towards the back of the court. I was literally occupying a 'front row seat'. I couldn't believe my luck, as I was facing, and was only a few yards away from, the witness box. I also discovered, in my eagerness, that if I leaned forward and looked to my right I could bypass the partition and screen and get a clear view of the whole court.

This didn't last long, as I quickly caught the attention of Judge Thackray. After the jury had left, he asked me to avoid looking at them, as on occasions they can feel intimidated by people staring at them. I apologised, stating that it wasn't intentional, and offered to move back one row to the only unoccupied row of seats. The judge accepted this offer; so, with all eyes on me, I stood up and took the seat immediately behind, and had to observe through the smoked-glass screen like everybody else. I'd done what I had desperately wanted to avoid doing: I had drawn attention to myself. I could tell that the family were uncomfortable with my sitting so close to them, but where else could I sit?

A jury has been used to decide on a defendant's guilt or innocence since before the Norman Conquest, and this practice is often said to be the cornerstone of the criminal justice system. In modern times, every defendant has the right to be tried by a jury for all but the most minor offences, but the vast majority of cases are heard in the magistrates' court. The most serious 'indictable only' crimes are always dealt with in the Crown Court, and if the defendant pleads not guilty and a trial is needed, a jury is required to decide their fate. In simple terms, the judge decides on the law and the jury decides on the facts. In reality, a jury is required in less than 1% of all court cases.

Juries are selected at random from the electoral register to create a sample of fellow citizens which represents a cross-section of society. Jurors must be aged eighteen or over and have no criminal record, but there is no upper age limit, although you can ask to be excused if you are aged over seventy. Currently, a judge must retire on reaching seventy years of age, regardless of their ability or physical fitness. So if you are over seventy you are deemed unfit to be a judge, but, apparently, deciding on guilt or innocence as part of a jury is fine. You need a very good excuse (such as mental or physical illness or disability) to avoid jury service. The requirement is to attend for ten working days, and your employer must allow you the time off but doesn't have to pay your wages. As at 2023, you can claim for lost earnings at the rate of £64.95 per day plus £5.71 for food and drink, and you can further claim for the cost of travel. For a seven-and-a-half-hour day, this works out at £8.66 an hour. So, for the very important and responsible 'job' of deciding on somebody's guilt or innocence in a murder trial, you are paid significantly less than the legally enforced minimum wage, which stands at £11.44 at the time of writing. However, this still works out at nearly £4,000 per week plus expenses for a twelve-person jury. Of course, most employers continue paying jurors' wages and save the taxpayer this expense.

Once all the people selected for jury service attend at court where a trial is about to begin, they are each allocated a number.

There then follows a draw in which twelve numbers are selected at random, and if your number is selected, you're on the jury. It is like a lottery. Each juror then takes their seat in the jury box and swears an oath or affirmation to say that they will faithfully consider the issues according to the evidence. In the privacy of the jury room they must select a foreperson, and after they have heard all the evidence it is the foreperson's job to chair the deliberations and deliver the verdict. What goes on in the jury room stays in the jury room. It would be a contempt of court for any of the jurors to ever reveal their discussions or share any details of their deliberations.

11

The Principle of Open Justice

In the next session, I again allowed the family members to enter the court before me, and on this occasion they spread themselves more thinly and occupied the second row of seats, leaving only the front row vacant. I think this was a deliberate tactic. I considered sitting on the seats reserved for police and officials or even among the family, but then decided to sit in my original seat on the front row and risk the wrath of the judge. I was very careful not to lean forward or fix my eyes on anybody for too long, and it seemed to do the trick.

The first day was very disjointed, with Judge Thackray repeatedly having to apologise to the jury for the long delays. I presume this was caused by the court being a judge short owing to sickness. I got the impression that the jury were getting a bit annoyed, and even the judge seemed embarrassed, at one stage saying, "I know you must be fed up of me saying this, but unfortunately we couldn't get started on time as I had other urgent business to attend to."

These repeated delays meant a late start, long breaks and an early finish, and this continued on the second day of the trial, which caused a lot of waiting around in the public area when the court wasn't sitting. You are never quite sure when you are going to be called back, so you need to stay close at hand. Buying a coffee or even visiting the toilet can be perilous, because you don't get long to take your seat in court, and it takes a brave person to enter the room when proceedings are already under way.

It was during one of the many breaks on the second day that a rather strange thing happened. I was approached by two plain-clothed police officers in the public area, who asked if they could "have a word". I followed them, but they couldn't find an office that was free, and so they took me into the court lobby. They didn't introduce themselves, but one of the officers, I later discovered when he gave evidence, was DC Stuart Quinn, the officer dealing with the case. The second officer, I presumed, was the family liaison officer (FLO).

The FLO said, "It's nothing to worry about, but can I ask what your interest is in this case?"

I replied, "I'm not worried, because I haven't done anything wrong and my interest is purely academic. Why do you ask?"

He said, "The family have spoken to me because they are concerned. They say that you keep staring at them."

I said, "Well, I am sensitive to their situation, but I haven't been staring at them. I've been trying to avoid them, but in such a small area it's impossible. I will try and sit well out of their way. The last thing I want to do is upset anybody."

He replied, "Thank you for your understanding." Off he went, no doubt to report back to the family. I was tempted to tell him that without my glasses I can barely see further than five yards, and if they were entitled to privacy perhaps there should be a room set aside for them.

I then considered the role of the FLO in all this. The post was created in the aftermath of the Macpherson report into the racist murder of Stephen Lawrence in 1993. The report was critical of the Metropolitan Police's dealings with the Lawrence family, and one of the recommendations was to have a dedicated FLO to improve communication between the investigating officers and the victim's family in cases of serious crime. In this instance, the FLO had the difficult job of dealing with a bereaved family who also happened to be the family of the defendant. As far as I am aware, all of the family members present were supporting Teresa, so Humberside Police were supporting the family of a defendant at the same time as helping to prosecute her. A difficult balancing act and a potential conflict of interest, I would say. This made me think back to my discussion with the FLO. I, as an impartial observer, was being asked by the police to respect the privacy of the family of the defendant in a murder case because they felt uncomfortable with *my* presence.

Following this discussion I did my best to keep out of their way, and concentrated on doing research on my phone and writing notes while in the open concourse. During the next session, I entered the court only to find that the family were now occupying all the front seats, and I had to take a seat at the back of the public gallery. That was fine by me, and in many ways provided a better view, but it seemed strange because they were all now sitting immediately in front of me when I was supposed to stop looking at them. I was being treated like an impostor who was gatecrashing a private event. Lord Atkinson certainly wasn't joking when he said that hearing a case in public was painful and humiliating.

After the first couple of days, with all the delays and setbacks it soon became clear that the trial would extend beyond the allotted five days. There were further conversations between the judge and counsel regarding the re-timetabling of sittings and the availability of witnesses, the judge, and the barristers themselves. The many discussions used up even more time. Sittings were sporadic, and there was one day (and several half-days) when the court didn't sit at all. In all honesty, the whole trial felt as if it had turned into a dog's dinner. I can't begin to imagine what the members of the jury were thinking.

12

The Prosecution Evidence

We heard prosecution evidence in the form of written statements read out by Alistair MacDonald. I have summarised what each of them said in the third person. It is worth remembering that this evidence was extracted from statements taken by the police shortly after the incident and had been agreed by the defence. This is not necessarily the order in which the evidence was given, but I have presented it in a way which is easier to follow.

Rachel Trafford

Rachel told us that she and her husband, Shaun, had been the Hansons' neighbours (occupying the adjoining house) for approximately two years, and that during that time she would occasionally hear "banging" from next door, which was more obvious in the summer, when the windows were open. She sometimes heard raised voices and doors being slammed and she could tell that Paul and Teresa had been arguing, although she couldn't make out the words because Paul and Teresa would be playing music. She said that Paul was a quiet and pleasant guy who kept himself to himself but would talk occasionally.

Shaun Trafford

Shaun stated that he had occasionally heard the Hansons arguing with each other over the past six months, which consisted of them both shouting. He had also heard Teresa say "Don't say that to me, don't speak to me like that." He said that the Hansons spent a lot of time in their garden all year round and were regularly in their hot tub playing music. He wouldn't say that they were alcoholics, but they enjoyed a drink.

He said that on the day of the incident he had got home at about 4pm, and at about 7.20pm he heard the "banging and slamming of internal doors" from next door, which lasted about ten minutes before it went quiet. There was then a significant time gap before he saw the ambulance arrive at the scene. As we now know, the incident happened much earlier than 7.20pm, so it appears that Mr Trafford was mistaken with his timings.

Michelle Harvey

Michelle was married to Teresa's brother and was visited by the Hansons on the day of the incident. The purpose of the visit was to give Michelle her birthday and Christmas presents. During their visit, Paul and Teresa told her about booking their holiday to Cape Verde and ordering their new car, which was due to be delivered in March 2023. They seemed in a good mood and left at about 2.30pm.

Andrew Hyland

After receiving the call at 7.08pm to attend 21 Little London Lane, the ambulance crew arrived at about 7.20pm and attempted to enter through the back door which leads directly to the kitchen-diner. Initially, they were unable to enter the property because the door was locked. When they eventually entered the house through the front door, they were greeted by Teresa (who was still on the telephone to the emergency services), and paramedic Andrew Hyland heard her say, "I've stabbed him." After being shown where Paul was lying, the paramedics began CPR. Teresa then said to them, "You lot are the experts and can save him. I'll give you £1,000 if you can." This comment was ignored, and the crew continued working on Paul for nearly half an hour before leaving at 7.50pm to take him to Hull Royal Infirmary. On arriving at 8.24pm, they handed him over to casualty staff. This time is at variance with the police officer and the doctor who both said the ambulance arrived at 8.20pm.

PC Adam Lazenby

At 7.16pm he received a report of a possible stabbing in West Cowick. He arrived and activated his body-worn camera at 7.33pm. After entering the property, he saw Paul on the kitchen/dining room floor in a large pool of blood, with the paramedics still working on him. Teresa was extremely distressed and was on the telephone to somebody – PC Lazenby believed it was her son. PC Lazenby asked her to come off the phone, and she said to him, "I didn't mean to do it," and then, "I didn't mean to do it. It was just an argument – I was making fucking tea." The officer then (at 7.35pm) arrested and cautioned her for Section 18 assault (this is Section 18 of the Offences Against the Person Act 1861, or 'grievous bodily harm with intent', as it is more commonly known) and placed her in handcuffs. Teresa's son, Ryan, arrived at the house moments before the ambulance left, and then Teresa was escorted to the police car and driven away.

En route to the police station, Teresa had what PC Lazenby described as a "panic attack" and he had to pull the car over at a nearby service station. After a short while she was transferred to a police van designed to transport prisoners and taken to Clough Road Police Station in Hull, arriving at 8.57pm. During the journey, PC Lazenby was informed that Paul had been pronounced dead at Hull Royal Infirmary and that he was in effect dead on arrival at 8.20pm. (There is a small discrepancy here with the time given by Andrew Hyland in his evidence.) PC Lazenby made the decision not to inform Teresa immediately, as is required under normal circumstances, because he believed it might cause her to have another panic attack, and there was nowhere to pull over now that they were on the M62 motorway.

They arrived at the police station at 8.57pm and Teresa was taken to a holding cell, where at 9.02pm PC Lazenby informed her of Paul's death and arrested her for his murder. He gave her the formal caution once again. In his evidence he stated that she made no reply to this, and that her only response was to scream. The court was then shown police bodycam footage of Teresa's arrest for murder while she was in the holding cell at Clough Road Police Station. As you might imagine, being informed of her husband's death at the same time as being arrested for murder sparked a hysterical reaction from Teresa. She responded by shouting "No!" and followed this with high-pitched screaming. It was quite harrowing to watch.

Dr Paul Stewart

Dr Stewart was on duty at Hull Royal Infirmary when he received a 'pre-alert call' from the ambulance service at 7.50pm (presumably as the ambulance was leaving the scene), at which time the patient was in a state of pulseless electrical activity. This is when a person's heart stops because the electrical activity is too weak to make it beat. Dr Stewart later received an update to say that Paul was now in a state of no electrical activity. The ambulance arrived at 8.20pm and the patient was transferred to the care of the hospital. Dr Stewart examined him and confirmed that there was no heartbeat and no electrical activity. He was of the opinion that further attempts at resuscitation would be futile, and at 8.24pm he declared Paul Hanson dead.

Kathryn Bird

On 2 February 2023, in her capacity as a forensic scientist Ms Bird examined a black-handled kitchen knife that was recovered at the scene. On it she found traces of Paul's blood and DNA, and a "distribution of blood and fatty deposits on the blade in keeping with a stabbing". She also examined the clothing worn by Paul at the time of the incident, consisting of a black Lacoste T-shirt, a black Hugo

Boss zip-fronted top and a pair of black Nike jogging bottoms. Ms Bird stated that the T-shirt and top "both bear single horizontal cuts measuring between 1.1 and 1.2 centimetres in length". She was of the opinion (expert witnesses are permitted to offer their opinion in evidence) that these cuts were made by "an item with a single cutting edge". She further stated that the tops were heavily bloodstained from the inside. She also examined the jogging bottoms and found that they were heavily bloodstained in the "lap area". In her opinion, based on the nature and position of the bloodstains, the victim "did not remain upright for any length of time unless a towel or similar item had been applied to the chest".

The 999 calls

All emergency telephone calls go through a generic call taker before being diverted to the appropriate service, and they are all recorded. What is said during these calls (which normally take place shortly after a serious incident) can be very distressing but also revealing – not just in *what* is said, 'in the heat of the moment' and without the benefit of legal advice, but also in the *way* it is said and in any voices or noises that can be heard in the background. In addition, if time or location are in dispute, there can be no argument about the timing of the call. The location of the caller is quickly established, whether by tracing a landline or by pinging their mobile phone. The caller's identity is usually confirmed by them giving their details. However, if somebody wishes to remain anonymous or pretends to be someone else, the phone they are using and, ultimately, voice recognition later in the investigation can prove their identity.

In this case, there was no dispute about the location or the timing of the emergency call, nor about the person making it. Teresa made the first 999 call on her mobile phone from her house at 7.05pm, following the incident. A recording of the conversation was played to the court, and it was extremely impactive. Even if a professional actor had read from a transcript, it would not have had anything like the dramatic effect that the real call recording had on the court. This was not somebody recalling events from the witness box; this was a recording of a live event as Paul was dying on the dining room floor. There can be no dispute about what was said, and the panic and distress were very real. That first telephone call lasted six minutes and forty-eight seconds, and it was impossible to write contemporaneous notes of the whole conversation, but I wrote as much as I could, covering all the main points, occasionally by summarising but mainly with direct quotes. The following is taken directly from my notes on the calls. I cannot possibly recreate in written form the drama of listening to the call live.

At 7.05pm, after establishing which service is required, Teresa is put through to the ambulance service. There is a delay of about one and a half minutes while a recorded message is played before the ambulance service answer the phone. During this time, Teresa can be heard shouting in the background.

TERESA HANSON: Paul, wake up, please wake up! Fuck! Paul, wake up, please!

It seems completely incongruous, but music plays in the background during most of the call. Then the call is answered.

TH: We had an argument and I stabbed him.

CALL TAKER: Who was it that stabbed him?

TH: It was just out of anger. I was just making fucking tea.

The call taker establishes Teresa's name and address, etc., then it all goes quiet and all that can be heard is the sound of a phone dialling. I am assuming that at this point the call taker was dispatching an ambulance to attend the address, which ties in with the statement of the paramedic who received the call at 7.08pm.

CT: Hello? Hello?

TH: Hello.

CT: When did this happen?

TH: About five minutes ago.

CT: Is there any serious bleeding?

TH: Lots and lots.

CT: Is he unconscious?

TH: Half and half.

CT: What did you stab him with?

TH: A little kitchen knife.

CT: Is it still in his chest?

TH: No. His legs are bent over like he fell over backwards.

The call taker takes Paul's details and gives advice regarding his care before the call drops out after six minutes and forty-eight seconds. This puts the time at about 7.12pm. At 7.14pm Teresa makes a second 999 call and, despite requesting the ambulance service once again, is put through to the police.

TH: Ambulance?

CT: Do you need the police?

TH: I don't think so. You can come if you like.

We know from the evidence of PC Lazenby that at this point (7.16pm) he received the call to attend the address.

CT: What happened?

TH: I was cooking tea, we had an argument, and I accidentally stabbed him.

CT: What?

TH: He told me to fuck off and called me a bitch so I…I don't know what I did.

CT: What injuries has he got?

TH: A chest wound.

CT: Was it a kitchen knife?

TH: Yes. Paul!

The sound of what seems like slapping can be heard in the background.

CT: Which room is he in?

TH: Dining room.

CT: Is he conscious and breathing?

TH: No…I don't know.

CT: Is he bleeding?

TH: Paul! Paul!

Sound of slapping.

TH: He's foaming at the mouth! Paul, look at me!

Sound of slapping. The call taker then takes Teresa and Paul's details.

CT: Where did you stab him?

TH: In the chest – it was an accident. My battery's running out. Please, he's going purple!

CT: I know.

TH: What do you mean, you know?

The ambulance arrives and the crew try to enter through the back door, only to find it locked. They then go to the front door and enter the house. Again, this ties in with the evidence of the paramedic, who arrived at 7.20pm and actually entered the house at 7.22pm.

TH: Come in, come in!

CT: Are ambulance inside your house now?

TH: Yeah. Oh, I can't believe this! [*To the ambulance crew*] Oh, please save him!

CT: We're on our way as well. [*Referring to the police.*]

TH: Yeah, fine. [*To the ambulance crew, in a muffled voice*] £1,000… Come on, guys.

Having dispatched a police patrol and satisfied herself that the ambulance is in attendance, the call taker ends the call.

This second call lasted approximately sixteen minutes, so it would have ended at around 7.30pm. We know that the police arrived shortly afterwards, by which time Teresa was on the phone to her son, Ryan. This is confirmed in Ryan's testimony, as he tells the court that he went straight to his mother's house and arrived moments before the ambulance left at 7.50pm.

It is impossible to replicate the sense of panic, distress and overwhelming horror as these events unfolded. I hope these brief excerpts can at least give you an indication of the sheer chaos of the situation. After we listened to the recording, there was a hush across the court as the grim reality began to sink in. We had just heard the soundtrack of a man dying, accompanied by live commentary. I don't think it is an exaggeration to say that the court as a whole was in a kind of stunned silence. The jury seemed to be in shock. The family seemed not to have heard the recording before; understandably, they were upset. The police, the barristers and the judge looked unmoved; some would have heard it before, and perhaps become a little desensitised. Teresa, as you would expect, was sobbing after being made to relive those terrible events.

There was a timely break while people composed themselves and reflected on what they'd just heard. During this time I wondered about the admissibility of some of the evidence from the recording. The second time Teresa called 999, she asked for the ambulance service but was put through to the police. It is not known if this was deliberate or the result of a misunderstanding.

Immediately after a police officer had been dispatched, the call taker asked Teresa, "What happened?"

If the call taker didn't already suspect that a crime had been committed at this stage, then surely Teresa's reply – "I was cooking tea, we had an argument, and I accidentally stabbed him" – would have removed any doubt. At this point, if not earlier, she should have been cautioned. The Police and Criminal Evidence Act 1984 (PACE) says:

A person whom there are grounds to suspect of an offence...
must be cautioned before any questions about an offence...

It doesn't matter that the call taker is not a police officer, nor that the questions were put to Teresa over the telephone. In my opinion, the subsequent questions constituted an interview. She was asked about the weapon, the circumstances and even "Where did you stab him?" The ambulance was en route and these questions weren't designed to assist medically, so what was their purpose?

The definition of an interview under PACE is "the questioning of a person regarding their involvement or suspected involvement in a criminal offence or offences." Unless there are exceptional circumstances, it must always be carried out under caution, must take place at a police station, and the suspect has the right to have a solicitor present.

I am not suggesting that any of this would have been possible under the circumstances, and I am certainly not criticising the call taker. What I did wonder was whether, as these safeguards were not in place for Teresa, her answers, which were significant, should have been admitted in evidence. I am not legally qualified, but if I were, and if I were representing Teresa, I would have made a submission to this effect. Maybe her legal team did attempt to have this part of the phone call ruled inadmissible but it was rejected. We will never know.

Dr Michael Parsons

The first live witness to give evidence for the prosecution was Dr Michael Parsons, who is a Home Office-registered forensic pathologist for the region. He was in his mid-forties, about five feet ten inches tall, with short, straight greying hair, of slim build and wearing a light grey suit. He was very professional and assured while giving his evidence. Softly spoken, very humble and polite, he told the court of his findings, always directing his answers to the jury. He had the air of a man who had given evidence of this nature many times before, and a quick Internet search confirms that he had indeed given evidence on numerous previous occasions in both Coroner's Courts and Crown Courts in cases of homicide like this one. After swearing the oath and introducing himself, he listed all of his professional qualifications and said that he had been performing the role of a forensic pathologist for about ten years and dealt with approximately ninety cases per year.

Dr Parsons told the court that he had performed a post-mortem in the mortuary at Hull Royal Infirmary. He had examined the body of Paul Hanson, and explained that the death was caused by a single stab wound to the chest, 129 centimetres (four feet three inches) from the heel of Paul's foot. He then went on to give the exact medical details of how death occurred. As Dr Parsons was an expert witness, he was allowed to give his opinion. He informed the court that, taking into consideration all the medical evidence and the circumstances, although the possibility of Paul dying as a result of an accidental stabbing could not be entirely excluded, it was, in his opinion, "highly unlikely" that he had simply walked onto the blade.

This is, of course, only a brief summary of the evidence given by Dr Parsons. I will cover his testimony in much more detail later in this book.

Ryan Hanson

As a member of the family attending the court on a daily basis in support of his mother, you may be wondering why Teresa's son gave evidence for the prosecution and his sister gave evidence on behalf of the defence. I wondered the same. While she was detained at the police station, Teresa, following legal advice, gave a prepared statement accusing her husband of being verbally and mentally abusive towards her over a number of years. It would appear that she was already laying the ground for her defence, or at least mitigation, by giving the impression that she had been the victim of domestic abuse. Of course, this was done without the knowledge of her son, as she was in custody at the police station and communication between them would not have been permitted.

It was while his mother was being detained that Ryan gave his first statement to the police, and it painted a rather different picture. I have no way of knowing whether or not Teresa was a victim of domestic abuse. If she was, there would normally be some kind of corroborative evidence to support this claim, such as police incident logs or records from other agencies. But, other than the evidence from the Hansons' neighbours about their occasional volatile arguments, nobody appears to have witnessed any form of domestic abuse. Even Teresa herself never alleged that she was the victim of any kind of physical violence. Domestic abuse might be emotional or physical, or both, but Ryan's evidence appeared to undermine any abuse-based argument.

Ryan, a thirty-two-year-old quantity surveyor, was, like his parents, shorter than average and of stocky build. He had short dark hair, was casually dressed, and spoke in a quiet voice. Not surprisingly, he appeared very nervous in the witness box. After taking the oath, he described his parents' relationship. He was questioned by the prosecuting barrister, Alistair MacDonald. He told the jury that his childhood was "the best" and that he was considered to have "cool parents". His father had built him and his sister a swimming pool in their back garden when they lived in Rawcliffe. He further stated that in all his life he didn't remember a "cross word" between his parents, and that they were "very much in love and it showed". His father "would do anything for his children and grandchildren".

Unusually for me, I genuinely felt a bit emotional. In my notes I wrote: "Heartbreaking: having to give evidence about the killing of your father by your mother." Whatever happened, Ryan was an innocent party who, clearly, loved his parents, and in an instant his world had come crashing down around him. He was a decent man and, following these events, appeared broken.

He then talked specifically about his father, saying that he had always "liked a drink" and that he "worked hard and played hard". He said that after Paul suffered his brain injury in 2010, he got drunk much more quickly and regularly fell asleep by 8pm. During the first Covid lockdown, Ryan had separated from his partner, the mother of his children, and had come to live with his parents for a period of six to nine months. He had joint custody of his children, who would also spend a lot of time at his parents' house. Ryan said that in all that time, he never witnessed any arguments or bickering. He had since met a new partner and at the time of the incident was living away from his parents. He told the court that his parents' world revolved around their grandchildren, and that on the evening before the incident his dad had been actively entertaining Ryan's two young sons. He had been impersonating a famous YouTube gamer, with an exaggerated American accent and generally acting the fool, much to his grandsons' amusement. Afterwards they had ordered a takeaway meal and watched a film, and as usual Paul had fallen asleep at about 8pm.

Ryan's evidence then moved on to the night of the incident. He said that he had received a phone call from his mother, who was hysterical and incoherent. He had to call her back, and afterwards went round to the house with his partner.

Ryan was then cross-examined by the defence counsel, Jason Pitter. This seemed more like a second chapter of evidence in chief than a cross-examination. Perhaps this was because Ryan had later given a second statement that was more favourable to the defence. Of course, he was supporting his mother and so was really on the side of the defence. However, he was not considered to be a hostile witness, where the roles would be reversed and he'd be treated as a defence witness and cross-examined by the prosecution. Unusually, he was allowed to sit in court before giving his evidence, which is an indication of his neutral status. He told the jury that he hadn't taken sides, as he loved both his parents equally. He has a pair of cufflinks and his mum has a ring, both made from his father's ashes. He said that Paul and Teresa were soulmates who were inseparable, besotted with each other, and he had (having separated from the mother of his children) been jealous of their close and happy relationship.

Ryan then told the court about his father's difficult relationship with his stepfather. Paul's biological father had died when Paul was young, and Teresa would encourage Paul to make the effort to see his mum, who, Paul believed, had sided with her husband. Ryan admitted his father could be short-tempered, but blamed the brain injury he had suffered when he was the victim of a serious assault in 2010.

Ryan completed his evidence by saying that before the incident, his parents had been looking forward to the future, having booked a summer holiday and ordered a new car. When asked what he thought about the idea of his mother wanting to hurt his father, he replied: "Impossible."

That is a summary of what Ryan had to say in evidence. It appears to be incompatible with what Teresa said in the prepared statement she gave while detained by the police. Ryan was giving evidence for the prosecution in order to refute this claim, and this is the likely reason why Teresa was forced to eventually give an alternative explanation for what had happened. It is worth remembering that she was on bail leading up to the trial and her conditions didn't include not communicating with her family. She did have a condition not to discuss the case, but this would be very difficult to enforce.

DC Stuart Quinn

DC Stuart Quinn was a detective from Humberside Police's Major Crime Team, and was the nominated officer in the case for this incident. He explained his role as directing and coordinating the investigation, although overall responsibility fell to the senior investigating officer, DCI Nicola Burnett.

DC Quinn went through the sequence of events and the timings of Teresa's initial arrest, arrival at the police station, and second arrest for murder once they were aware of her husband's death. He also confirmed that she had no previous convictions and was of good character.

Shortly after her arrival at the police station, Teresa was examined by a healthcare professional (a nurse), who noted that she had sustained no injuries and declared her fit to be detained.

When a suspect arrives at a police station they are 'booked in' and given their rights. These include:

- to consult with a solicitor and receive independent legal advice free of charge
- to have someone informed of their arrest
- to consult the 'codes of practice' which outline their rights while in detention.

DC Quinn informed the court that Teresa had exercised her right to consult with a solicitor, to receive legal advice, and to have him or her present while she was interviewed. Unless there are exceptional circumstances, a suspect cannot be interviewed without receiving legal advice and having a solicitor present unless they make it clear that they don't want or need this. (Even then, the police have to enquire as to why they have declined the services of a solicitor.)

Due to the lateness of the hour and, I presume, to allow the police time to make further enquiries into the incident, Teresa wasn't interviewed until the following day (Thursday 29 December). The solicitor arrived at Clough Road Police Station – except she wasn't a solicitor. Although she was employed by a legitimate firm of solicitors, she was merely an accredited legal representative. I found it surprising that in a case as serious as murder, a senior solicitor – or any kind of solicitor – was not dispatched. But then again, I imagine that availability was an issue late at night in the Christmas holiday period, and especially with the system of legal aid funding, in which attending a police station is often regarded by solicitors as a 'loss leader'. I imagine it's a sign of the times – the same as the police officer dealing with a murder being of the rank of constable.

The routine practice for a solicitor arriving at a police station is to ask the interviewing officer for 'disclosure'. DC Quinn gave evidence to say that the minimum the police must disclose is what their client has been arrested for and the grounds for that arrest. Of course, the solicitor will always want more. Disclosure is a bit of a tactical game: the solicitor wants to know as much information as possible from the police, to assess how much evidence they have and to advise their client accordingly. The police, meanwhile, want to disclose as little as possible, as they are afraid that the suspect will give an account during interview that safely negotiates its way around the evidence. It is like a game of poker: both sides want an idea of the strength of their opponent's hand before deciding which cards to play. If the police provide only the minimum disclosure, it often results in a 'no comment' type of interview. Sometimes it is in the police's interest to disclose nearly everything, particularly if the evidence is overwhelming. This tells the solicitor that their client is likely to be charged regardless of what they say in interview, so the suspect will then go down the path of damage limitation by cooperating, hoping to make the best of a bad job.

DC Quinn told the court that he had prepared a disclosure document and handed it to the legal representative, who then had a private consultation with Teresa. DC Storey was the interviewing officer, and the accepted procedure is to introduce everyone, read the suspect's rights and then begin the interview. All interviews at a police station are audio- or video-recorded onto a disc or a hard drive, and the suspect and their solicitor are entitled to a copy.

Following a long consultation with her legal representative, Teresa had been advised to give what is known as a 'prepared statement'. This is a tactic used more and more by solicitors, in which they try to perform a balancing act between making sure that their client doesn't reveal too much information and avoiding the possibility of 'adverse inferences' being drawn later at court. (More of this later.) The prepared statement was read out in the interview by Teresa's legal representative. It said:

> *Over the years, my husband has been verbally and mentally abusive to me. The injury occurred whilst I was holding the knife when he walked onto it. At no time did I intend to kill him or cause him serious harm.*

This may not be word perfect, as we didn't get to see a written copy of the statement, but it is certainly the essence of it. As you can see, it is a short statement which claims that Paul walked onto the knife while she was holding it, and the only context is that she had suffered years of verbal and mental abuse. This seems to be a curious mix. On the one hand, she appears to be going down the route of self-defence or provocation by alleging that she was the victim of long-term abuse. At the same time, she seems to be claiming that it was a complete accident. If it was an accident, surely the allegation of abuse would not be relevant?

The interviewing officer confirmed with Teresa that this was her statement and that she had read and understood it. Teresa signed the statement at 2.48pm on Thursday 29 December 2022. The interview continued, with the interviewing officers asking numerous questions about the incident itself and the circumstances surrounding it. Each received a reply of "no comment". DC Quinn informed us that Teresa was interviewed on two further occasions – at 6.30pm on the same evening, and again the following day. Each time, she gave a prepared statement to say that she had nothing further to add to her previous statement, and then replied "no comment" to all subsequent questions. She was charged with murder at 9.53pm on Friday 30 December 2022, and appeared at Hull Magistrates' Court the following morning. As they had detained her for more than thirty-six hours (the maximum time allowed), I am assuming that the police had been granted an extension warrant by the magistrates.

DC Quinn was then cross-examined by Jason Pitter, who merely confirmed some of the details of his testimony, but as most of the evidence was factual, it wasn't contested.

This concluded the prosecution evidence.

13

The Caution

During her time in police custody, Teresa would have been cautioned on at least six occasions: her two arrests, her three interviews, and finally when she was charged. In all probability, she was cautioned several times more at various stages of her detention. The court was told by DC Quinn that on each occasion she was interviewed, not only was Teresa cautioned but the meaning of the caution was explained to her and she confirmed that she understood. This would have taken place in the presence of her legal representative, who, I am sure, also explained the meaning and significance of the caution during their private consultations.

Before the caution was changed under the Criminal Justice Act 1994, it was:

> *You do not have to say anything unless you wish to do so,*
> *but what you say may be given in evidence.*

This was a straightforward right of silence, with a warning that if you chose to talk, it might be used against you in evidence.

The new caution came into being on 10 April 1995. What brought about the change was the common practice of suspects remaining silent when interviewed by police, which is still their right. However, once charged, if the suspect is to be prosecuted, the police must disclose their evidence to the defence. At this stage the suspect would then be in the advantageous position of knowing the full extent of the evidence against them, and they would be able to tailor their alibi or defence accordingly and then give it as evidence in court. The prosecution had no advance warning of the suspect's intended testimony, so couldn't disprove or refute their evidence. This was known as 'the ambush defence'. In order to close this loophole and prevent the same thing from happening in the future, the wording of the caution changed to:

> *You do not have to say anything. But it may harm your defence if you do not mention when questioned something which you later rely on in court. Anything you do say may be given in evidence.*

In simple terms, this means that the accused still retains their right to silence. However, if they choose not to answer police questions, any evidence that is used in their defence in court may be treated with suspicion if it is something they could have reasonably told the police at the time of their arrest. Of course, the defendant does not have to give evidence in court at all. Furthermore, under the Criminal Procedure and Investigations Act 1996, the defence must submit a 'defence statement' within twenty-eight days of the disclosure of the prosecution evidence in a Crown Court trial. So, once they have sight of the prosecution case against them, if they intend to plead not guilty to the charge, they must inform the prosecution of the basis for their defence. This gives the police the opportunity to check the validity of the defence's evidence before the trial.

In the case of Teresa Hanson, her legal team submitted her defence statement on Wednesday 31 May 2023 (less than a fortnight before the trial), after receiving full disclosure of the prosecution evidence against her. Excerpts from this were read out in court, but no printed copy was available. I can't say that what follows is exactly what it said, but it was along the lines of:

> *Whilst preparing tea, I was chopping onions and Paul came into the kitchen, calling me names. I turned to push him away, forgetting I was holding a knife, and accidentally stabbed him. It wasn't until afterwards that I realised he was injured.*

You will notice that this statement is significantly different from the one Teresa gave at the police station. Her account of what happened has changed from Paul walking onto the knife to her pushing him away with a knife in her hand. The claim of suffering abuse over the years has completely disappeared. The only common theme is that the injury was an accident.

You may well ask: if it was a pure accident, why didn't she say this at the time and explain the circumstances fully to the police when she was interviewed? Was it merely a coincidence that this 'accident' occurred during, or immediately after, a row with her husband? If it had been a different type of accident (such as fatally injuring him while cutting down a tree with a chainsaw, for example), she would still have been interviewed by the police. Would she have been advised by her solicitor to give no comment, or would she have given a full and detailed account? Teresa's decision to issue the police with a prepared statement at the police station and then refuse to answer any subsequent questions was made, I imagine, based on the advice of her accredited legal representative. Was this good advice? What was the reason for giving it? All legal advice is subject to 'legal privilege' and is strictly confidential (like a doctor/patient relationship), so we will never know for sure.

So what happened in between these times that caused Teresa to significantly alter her account? We can't be certain, but it probably had something to do with the fact that by then her legal team had

had sight of the prosecution evidence. This, of course, included the statement of Dr Parsons, who said that it was "highly unlikely" that an injury of the type sustained by Paul could have been caused by him walking onto the knife. Dr Parsons' evidence also revealed that the stab wound was 129 centimetres (four feet three inches) from the heel of Paul's foot. Assuming he was upright at the time, this suggested that the knife was held at shoulder height by Teresa, who is 155 centimetres (five feet one inch) tall. Why would she be holding a knife at shoulder height? This would make her claim of Paul walking onto it a bit more difficult to believe. The disclosure would also have included the statement from Ryan, who said that his parents had never had a "cross word", which undermined Teresa's claim of being a victim of verbal and mental abuse – a claim which was now absent from her defence.

During her three police interviews, Teresa would have been asked numerous detailed questions about the incident, which she refused to answer. The police have a duty to ask every possible question to try to establish what happened. They don't give it up as a pointless exercise just because the only response they receive is "no comment". This is because the caution says "if you do not mention *when questioned*" (my italics), so the suspect has to be questioned in detail to avoid the excuse of 'I was never asked – if they had asked me, I would have told them', which would allow the suspect to get round the requirements of the caution.

I was astonished that the transcripts from those interviews were not used as part of the prosecution evidence. You may think that there was no point, as Teresa refused to answer any of the questions. I am not suggesting that the complete transcripts from all three interviews should have been read out word for word, as that would soon have sent the audience (the jury) to sleep, but I do think that reading out excerpts quoting the most relevant questions would have put into sharp focus the contrast between Teresa's refusal to answer the most simple and straightforward questions about the incident at the time and her later detailed explanation as to exactly what took place in her statement, made only after the prosecution evidence had been disclosed.

14

Adverse Inferences

The jury didn't have the benefit of listening to the police interviews or even seeing transcripts of them, but during the interviews Teresa would have been given the opportunity for 'free recall' – an explanation of events in her own words. She would then have been asked open questions (who, what, when, where, why and how), followed by specific closed questions ('did you…?', 'have you…?', etc.), and, finally, leading questions ('you did, didn't you?') along the following lines:

- You said in your prepared statement that he walked onto the knife. Tell me exactly how that happened.
- How long was it before you called an ambulance?
- You said in the 999 call that you stabbed him "out of anger". What did you mean?
- What was the row about?
- What did you use to stab him?
- Where did you stab him?
- Why did you stab him?
- Where was the knife immediately before you used it to stab him?
- What did Paul do after you had stabbed him?
- Did you call 999 immediately after stabbing him?
- Did you intend to injure him?

- You knew that if you stabbed him in the chest he would at least be seriously injured, didn't you?
- You had a row, lost your temper and deliberately stabbed him in the chest, didn't you?

These are just some of the questions that *may* have been asked by the police, each of which would have been answered with a simple "no comment". Teresa was in a position where she could have reasonably been expected to answer most if not all of these questions, or even deny certain things or give an alternative explanation. On legal advice, she chose not to.

Section 34 of the Criminal Justice and Public Order Act 1994 says (my emphasis):

> *Where, in any proceedings against a person for an offence, evidence is given that the accused—*
> *(a) at any time before he was charged with the offence, on being questioned under caution by a constable trying to discover whether or by whom the offence had been committed, **failed to mention any fact relied on in his defence** in those proceedings; or*
> *(b) on being charged with the offence or officially informed that he might be prosecuted for it, failed to mention any such fact...*
> *being a fact which in the circumstances existing at the time the accused could reasonably have been expected to mention when so questioned [or] charged...the court or jury, in determining whether the accused is guilty of the offence charged, may draw such inferences from the failure as appear proper.*

So if a suspect fails to mention any fact during a police interview (or when being charged) which they later rely on for their defence at a trial, on the judge's direction the jury may draw adverse inferences when deciding whether or not the suspect is guilty.

Defendants cannot be compelled to give evidence in their own defence. It is for the prosecution to prove their case. In this particular case, however, without Teresa giving evidence it would be difficult to imagine how a jury would be convinced that the stabbing was an accident and then find her not guilty. If you remember, the only points at issue in this trial were:

- that the action that caused Paul's death was deliberate
- that there was an intention to cause at least really serious harm.

The prosecution evidence of the 999 calls and the testimony from Dr Parsons was quite convincing, so the only person who could possibly refute that evidence and persuade a jury that Paul's death was a terrible accident was Teresa herself.

15

The Reporters

After a few days of attending the court, I had started to get to know some of the reporters who visited occasionally. There were representatives from the BBC, independent news channels and the local papers. One reporter even listened remotely on behalf of the Press Association. Journalists are curious by nature, and initially I think they wanted to check me out. Maybe they thought I was connected to the family in some way but wondered why I kept myself to myself. Perhaps they thought there was a split in the family in terms of their support for Teresa and that there was a story to be found there. Some even thought I was a fellow journalist.

They weren't anything like the stereotypical red-top tabloid reporter you might imagine. With one exception they were quite open and friendly, and it changed my perception of journalists. I think it helped when I told them that I was a former police officer, and it also helped that (I like to think) I looked quite respectable. Once I had gained their trust they were quite happy to chat to me and discuss various aspects of the case. It became mutually beneficial because, from my point of view, I found it interesting to learn about their job and how they went about reporting the case. From their point of view, I could help by updating them as to what had happened in their absence and letting them know when the next session was due to start. They were busy people covering all kinds of different stories, including the doctors' strike, which was the main news at the time. I think it was nice to have somebody to talk to who wasn't involved with the case, and it helped pass the time for all of us. Two of them even gave me their phone numbers so I could let them know what time the hearing would resume. This enabled them to plan their day and cover other stories.

I wrongly assumed that they were all local, but I discovered that some of them covered the whole of the Yorkshire region and lived fifty or sixty miles from Hull. I was conscious that they had a job to do and had very little spare time, with tight deadlines to write a report for their news outlet's website that evening or even a television report for the late afternoon. I could tell that they were under pressure and I didn't want to be a nuisance, but they were generous with their time. They told me about their job and how difficult it could be. I learned that they were the same as everybody else. They grumbled about their job, the internal politics, the unpredictability and the subsequent childcare problems. It sounded very similar to being a police officer.

On one occasion, one of the television reporters had been unexpectedly diverted from covering the doctors' strike at Leeds General Infirmary, where a picket line had formed and protests were under way. Originally they had been doing a written report for a website and taking a few photographs. The reporter lived nearby, and had gone straight to the hospital. They were then told by their producer to go straight to Hull Crown Court, as Teresa Hanson was about to give evidence and the producer needed a report for the evening television news. The reporter was horrified, as they couldn't appear on television dressed in such a casual outfit. They spent their entire lunchtime visiting charity shops, and eventually bought a smart jacket from Oxfam for £5, which they couldn't reclaim on their expenses. That night I watched the news bulletin starring the £5 charity jacket, and thought the reporter looked very smart. Who would ever know?

On another occasion, a different reporter got fed up of hanging around, and told me they were popping out to Tesco (about 100 metres along the road) for a sandwich. They asked me if I would give them a call if anything happened. I was quite happy to do this, as I might want a similar favour on another day. Of course, as soon as they left the building, the inevitable happened. "The case of Teresa Hanson," the usher called, and everybody walked quickly into court. I decided I wouldn't have time to call the reporter, so took my seat. Thankfully, I remembered reading that live texting from a courtroom was allowed. I sent a quick text, and the reporter made their way to the press bench shortly afterwards. The only thing they missed out on was the rest of their lunch.

I was very aware that other people involved in the case were noticing that I was occasionally sitting with the reporters and having long discussions. I'm sure the family were wondering what our relationship was and what we were talking about. They may have thought I was some kind of informant feeding the journalists information, when in reality we were probably talking about the weather or the price of petrol. This might have been the catalyst for what happened next.

During one of the many breaks, I was alone and about to take a seat in the public concourse when I saw the defence counsel, Jason Pitter, walking towards me. I wondered where he was going, as he was walking in the opposite direction to the barristers' offices. Much to my surprise, he walked straight up to me and, with a smile, asked me what my interest was in the case. I guess by this time, several days into the trial, he realised that it wasn't just passing curiosity: I was here for the duration and was speaking to reporters.

I would imagine that court staff are used to people 'popping in' to see what's happening after reading about a case in the paper or hearing about it on the news. They almost certainly get bored after a few hours of hanging around during the many breaks, followed by short sessions consisting mainly of legal arguments and the reading of statements and only occasionally hearing live testimony. They then go home after deciding that it is much easier to read about the case online or in the papers.

I don't know whether Mr Pitter was acting on behalf of the family, who may have been annoyed by my continued presence, or whether he was genuinely curious about this strange man attending every session and writing lots of notes. He was very polite and friendly, so I told him that my interest was purely academic and I was particularly keen on learning about adverse inferences. At this point, Mr Pitter made his excuses and returned to his office; he would, no doubt, report back to the family later on.

Before the trial began, I had naively thought that I would go largely unnoticed or just be ignored. In a way I was flattered to receive such attention, but it demonstrated that the system of open justice was something that was not only tolerated but was also viewed with suspicion.

16

The Case for the Defence

Teresa Hanson

It was Friday 16 June, the fifth day of the trial and my fourth full day in attendance. During the week there were sometimes no reporters at all in court, or maybe one or two calling in now and again to check on the progress of the case. Today there were three or four reporters present.

After all the delays, legal arguments and waiting around, we were finally going to hear the crucial testimony. Teresa had already admitted to killing her husband. I was looking forward to hearing her evidence from the witness box, assessing her body language and seeing how she coped with the pressure. She could no longer answer 'no comment'; she would have to give an explanation as part of her evidence in chief and then be cross-examined by the prosecuting counsel. We had heard the prosecution evidence. A forensic pathologist had said that an accidental stabbing was "highly unlikely". The court had listened to the 999 calls in which Teresa herself had said that she had stabbed Paul "out of anger". As the defendant, she could not be compelled to give evidence in her own defence, but in the face of the prosecution evidence it seemed she effectively had no other option. Her whole future depended on the next few hours, and she needed to convince the jury that she was not guilty of murder. She had put all of her eggs in one basket labelled 'accident'. The offence of manslaughter was still an option for the jury, but they would have to come to the conclusion that although they believed the stab to Paul's chest to be a deliberate act, they didn't think Teresa intended to cause him serious harm. She was fighting for her future, and for the first time, nearly six months after the incident, we would hear at first hand Teresa's account of what had happened on that dreadful night.

This was going to be a monumental task, especially for somebody who had never given evidence in court before. The witness box is said to be the loneliest place in the world, and I can vouch for that, having been in that position many times, albeit for the prosecution. There is no solicitor to guide you, nobody to refer to, no opportunity to expand your answers, and no hiding place. It's just you, a court virgin, against a seasoned professional. The fact that Teresa would be questioned by a highly regarded and experienced barrister made things seem mismatched. It was as if a random person had been taken off the street, put into a boxing ring and told they had to go a few rounds with a professional boxer. You didn't want to miss it, but you watched through your fingers and cringed.

As Teresa was speaking in her own defence, she would first give her evidence in chief and be asked questions by her own barrister, Jason Pitter. As the name suggests, the evidence in chief is the witness's own account of what happened. Their barrister takes them through their evidence by asking open questions such as 'tell me what happened', 'was anybody else there?' and 'how did you feel?' They are not allowed to ask leading questions. A leading question is one which either suggests a particular answer or assumes an unestablished fact. Well-known examples of leading questions are 'when did you stop beating your wife?' and the famous question asked of Debbie McGee by Caroline Aherne's character, Mrs Merton, "What first, Debbie, attracted you to the millionaire Paul Daniels?"

Teresa entered the witness box looking pale, with her hair down, and wearing her familiar black top and trousers, and I could see that she was still wearing her wedding ring. In her left hand she held the card with the oath written on it, which served to exaggerate the trembling of her arm. In her right hand she held the Bible aloft. Not surprisingly, her voice wavered as she took the oath before settling down with the first few straightforward questions. I quickly looked around the court, and absolutely everybody in the room was transfixed.

In her evidence in chief, Teresa accepted that her actions had led to the death of her husband:

JASON PITTER: Did you mean to stab him?
TERESA HANSON: No.
JP: Did you intend to kill him?
TH: No, definitely not.
JP: Or cause serious harm?
TH: No.
JP: Or any harm?
TH: No.
JP: Have you ever wanted to hurt him?
TH: No!

She then broke down in tears and, after a short pause to compose herself, insisted that she was okay to carry on. I think the plan here was to establish absolute clarity from the beginning and to make an impact – and it certainly did that.

Mr Pitter then asked about her background. She told the court that she had met her husband when she was sixteen and that they had been together for a total of thirty-seven years. She had always worked – mostly as a self-employed hairdresser. They had two children together, Ryan and Sherri.

When asked about Paul's drinking, Teresa said that most of the time he was okay but on occasions he would 'click'. His mood would change from happy to angry if she mentioned his drinking.

She said she understood that his brain injury was responsible for his behaviour, and it didn't bother her.

She was then asked about the prepared statement she had made at the police station.

> JP: "Over the years, my husband has been verbally and mentally abusive."
> TH: I did say that.
> JP: Would he do it in front of people?
> TH: No.
> JP: Would you disagree with what Ryan said?
> TH: No.
> JP: Did you ever reach the stage where you didn't want to be together?
> TH: No, never.

Mr Pitter then went on to ask about the night in question.

> JP: Were you drunk?
> TH: No.
> JP: What was the mood like?
> TH: Good.
> JP: Did he ever drink when you weren't there?
> TH: He did secret drinking, yeah.

Teresa was asked about the build-up to the incident.

> TH: I asked him to wait till we'd had tea before drinking any more. He told me to shut up, called me a bitch and said he can drink what he likes.
> JP: Is that a word he'd use in front of other people?
> TH: No. He didn't normally use it to me.
> JP: What did you say?

TH: I told him not to talk to me like that.

JP: Was your voice raised as well?

TH: I probably shouted at him, yes.

JP: Then what happened?

TH: It was over in ten minutes. He slammed the door [*I assume she meant the back door, as they had an open-plan kitchen-diner*] and went back into the dining room.

JP: What were you doing?

TH: Cutting onions.

JP: What happened next?

TH: He walked back in, shouting, "I told you, I don't want tea, chuck it in the fucking bin!" I tried to push him out of my face.

She then gave a bizarre demonstration to the jury. Clutching a pen in her right hand to represent the knife, she turned 135 degrees to her left, raised her arms and pushed them out in front of her. With the pen remaining in a vertical position, it wasn't clear how the knife could have penetrated her husband's chest.

JP: What was your intention?

TH: To get him out of my face and carry on cooking.

JP: What did Paul do?

TH: He just walked away.

JP: Did he make any sound?

TH: No.

JP: Was there any music playing?

TH: Yes.

JP: What did you do then?

TH: I finished slicing the onions and put them in the pan.

JP: When did you first become aware something was wrong?

TH: When I heard the dog bark. I looked at the dog, saw blood on the floor, and saw Paul laid in the dining room.

JP: What did you think had happened?

TH: I don't know. I looked to see where the blood was coming from.

JP: Did you see where it was coming from?

TH: Eventually.

JP: Were you able to work out what had happened to him?

TH: Yes.

JP: What did you think had happened?

TH: I realised I must have accidentally stabbed him.

JP: Before then, did you realise the knife had gone into him?

TH: No.

JP: When you pushed him away, what were you feeling?

TH: I was angry.

JP: Did you want to stab him?

TH: No, I just wanted to push him away.

JP: Did you know you had a knife in your hand?

TH: I wasn't conscious of it.

JP: What did you do next?

TH: I rang the ambulance, did CPR and went to get a towel.

JP: Did you understand what had happened?

TH: I did after, but I don't know how.

JP: How were you feeling while making the 999 call?

TH: Scared, distraught.

JP: Were you thinking clearly?

TH: No.

After going through the arrival of the ambulance and her arrest by the police, she was asked about events at the police station. On her arrest for murder, which we had seen on the police bodycam video, Mr Pitter asked:

JP: What were you upset about?

TH: That Paul had died.

JP: How did you feel?

TH: Dead myself.

JP: What was your frame of mind?

TH: Not good.

JP: Why didn't you answer police questions?

TH: I was advised not to.

JP: Did it cross your mind not to listen to the advice given?

TH: No.

That concluded the evidence in chief of Teresa Hanson. It can be summarised as follows: she began by claiming that the elements necessary for murder were not present, i.e. it was not a deliberate act and there was no intention to kill or to do really serious (or any) harm. She then gave evidence to back up these claims:

1. Explaining her prepared statement and squaring it with Ryan's evidence.
2. Stating that she had never considered leaving Paul (to rule out any motive to hurt him).
3. Describing how her husband could turn nasty after a drink, through a combination of his brain injury and his excessive drinking (but stressing that she was sympathetic because of his condition).
4. Mentioning his 'secret' drinking habit, implying that on the night he may have had more to drink than she'd first realised.
5. Claiming that she was chopping onions at the time, in order to explain why she had a knife in her hand.
6. Telling the court that after the stabbing, Paul simply walked away without saying anything, and that there was music playing. She continued cooking the onions and didn't realise that anything was wrong until the dog barked. (This was to explain how the

freshly chopped onions were cooked by the time the police arrived.)

7. Admitting that she was angry with Paul and that she wasn't thinking straight when she made the 999 calls (to explain her "out of anger" comment).

8. Stating that she was so upset because her husband had died, not because she had been arrested for murder.

9. Explaining why she didn't give a full account to the police after her arrest by saying that her frame of mind was "not good" and she was merely following legal advice (so adverse inferences couldn't be drawn).

Although Teresa's testimony was fairly predictable, it raised several more important questions. There were lots of inconsistencies and gaps. Questions I would have liked to ask her were going through my mind one after the other. I imagine most of the jury members were feeling the same.

The next stage was going to be even more difficult for Teresa. Her evidence was to be cross-examined by the prosecuting counsel, Alistair MacDonald. I knew he would be well prepared and would ask many of the questions I wanted to hear answered. He was a distinguished barrister and this would be 'meat and drink' for him. Or so I thought.

The questions he asked were, in the end, fairly routine and predictable – the sort of questions Teresa's legal team would have anticipated – and were met with what you might call '*Blue Peter* answers' ("Here's one I prepared earlier"). The more incisive questions prompted replies such as "I can't remember", "it was all a blur", and the old favourite, "I don't know, I just panicked". These types of answers weren't followed up but just seemed to be accepted. The tumultuous climax I was expecting never happened. It seemed a bit of a half-hearted effort from Mr MacDonald and I suspect this was because he didn't want to cause Teresa any undue distress which might have caused the jury to be sympathetic towards her. Witnessing such a performance was like watching a football match in which a draw constitutes a good result for both teams, so the ball spends most of the time in midfield. Nobody wanted to go on the attack, for fear of being caught on the break.

I think most people present believed that what had happened was a genuine tragedy. On the evidence, it was difficult to make a case for it being a straightforward accident. On the other hand, I think people couldn't reconcile themselves with the idea of this middle-aged wife, mother and grandmother of previous good character being a murderer. But with the defendant adamant that the death was an accident, the prosecution *had* to pursue a murder conviction. There was no middle ground. The only way Teresa could be found guilty of manslaughter was for the jury to reach this alternative verdict; and after the judge's direction regarding the law on manslaughter, even this was difficult to imagine. The only possibility was if the jury had sufficient sympathy for Teresa to fudge it with a manslaughter conviction.

Sherri Hanson

Sherri was the twenty-nine-year-old daughter of Paul and Teresa, and she worked as a hairdresser. Earlier in the year her father had made a post on Facebook expressing his pride after she was nominated for a hairstyling award. She is the younger of the two children and, unlike Ryan, was appearing as a defence witness. As well as doing similar work to her mother, she also had a similar appearance, being slightly over five feet tall and of stout build, with long hair. She was smartly dressed, with her hair bleached a subtle blonde, and she was softly spoken. Not surprisingly, she appeared very nervous when giving evidence.

Even though Sherri was a defence witness, after taking the oath she more or less repeated what her brother had told the court:

- she said that her parents had always had a good relationship
- she had never seen her mother being aggressive towards her father
- the couple did everything together, and Teresa always worried about Paul.

After explaining how her mother had looked after and nursed her father back to health after his accident, and again following his assault, Sherri added that Teresa was always caring for Paul and thought the world of him, and it was awful to see how much pain she was in. Most couples don't have a perfect relationship, and we know from the neighbours' evidence that the Hansons 'had their moments'. It seemed that Sherri had laid it on a bit thick.

Finally, when asked about the possibility of her mother deliberately harming her father Sherri responded, "Impossible – she loved him too much." You may think 'impossible' was an unusual word choice, but her brother had used exactly the same word in his evidence.

Vanessa Lappin

I can only imagine that the reason for calling Vanessa Lappin as a witness was because of who she was (namely Paul Hanson's elder sister) rather than what she could tell us. She had no new evidence to offer, so I presume it was an attempt by the family to present a united front.

I don't have the details of Paul's extended family but I believe that, other than his children, Vanessa was his only blood relative to attend the trial and give evidence in support of Teresa. If Paul had any other living relatives, I presume they either refused to give a statement or were never asked. Either way, they didn't attend court, and this gave the impression that Teresa had 100% support from both sides of the family. This may well have been the case, but it was notable that her own brother didn't attend court in support or offer himself as a character witness. His wife, Michelle Harvey, did provide a statement, but it was submitted on behalf of the prosecution. Here I give a brief summary of what Vanessa had to say.

Aged fifty-eight, Vanessa was a tall, smartly dressed, well-built lady with long ash-coloured hair. She stated that she had been close to her brother and happy that he was married to Teresa. Vanessa had known Teresa for thirty-seven years – since Teresa and Paul began dating. She told the court how hard-working, kind and caring her sister-in-law was, and how grateful she (Vanessa) had been after they'd both helped her through a difficult time. She concluded by saying that Teresa was a wonderful mother to her children and was a doting grandmother.

There was no cross-examination of Sherri or Vanessa by Alistair MacDonald. Presumably he thought there was no value in it or there was nothing contentious in their evidence (and they were short of time). But if this was the case, why were they required to give evidence in person rather than have their statements read out in court like the other character witnesses? I can only speculate that the defence team decided to call them as live witnesses because Sherri's testimony would have the impact of the accused's daughter speaking from the heart, and because what Vanessa said would carry more weight as she was a close relative of the victim. Their evidence was followed by the reading of four other witness statements to the court. These were mainly from long-standing friends of the couple, and they gave further evidence of Teresa's good character.

In the absence of the jury, Mr MacDonald quite rightly raised the issue of Section 34 (adverse inferences) with Judge Thackray. I thought it would be a straightforward decision to invite the jury to draw their own conclusions as to why Teresa had given evidence in her own defence at court using information that she could have told the police, either during her interviews or after being charged, but chose not to. But to my utter amazement, Judge Thackray made the decision not to invite the jury to draw inferences. Surely this was exactly the situation for which the legislation was designed? He cited his reasons as being that Teresa was in shock and distress having learned that her husband had died (as could be seen from the police bodycam footage), and that she had refused to answer questions only because she was advised not to by her legal representative. Mr MacDonald seemed very accepting of this, but my jaw was on the floor. She was shocked because her husband had died? She was in custody for two days and interviewed three times, which I would have thought was sufficient time to compose herself and give a considered response to police questions. She was acting on legal advice? If this is a valid excuse, then every solicitor in the land will advise every suspect to refuse to answer questions. The only compensation for this was the thought that even without this direction, the jury would have sufficient intelligence to draw their own conclusions.

This marked the end of the defence case, and the jury had the weekend to consider (individually) all the evidence without the judge's direction on adverse inferences. In fact, they had a long weekend because, due to "existing commitments", the hearing wouldn't resume until Tuesday 20 June.

Over the weekend, Teresa's evidence was widely reported on the television news and in both local and national newspapers. The headlines all had a similar theme, along the lines of 'Grandmother stabbed husband with kitchen knife before carrying on chopping onions for dinner' or 'Hairdresser stabs husband to death and then uses same knife to cut onions'.

17

The Jury's Deliberations

Tuesday 20 June

The court reconvened on Tuesday, and the morning session was devoted to the closing speech for the prosecution, followed by the closing speech for the defence.

Alistair MacDonald reminded us of the evidence contained in the 999 call in which Teresa had said that she had stabbed her husband "out of anger". He also quoted the evidence given by Dr Parsons, who had said that an accidental stabbing was "highly unlikely". He then summarised the evidence of the forensic scientist, Kathryn Bird, who had said that it was likely that Paul did not remain upright for any length of time after the stabbing, and that she had found traces of his blood and fatty deposits on the knife when she had examined it. Mr MacDonald invited the jury to consider how likely it was that Teresa didn't realise that she had stabbed Paul or notice that he'd collapsed to the floor, or that she went on to finish chopping onions with the same bloodstained knife. Finally, he reminded the jury of Teresa's prepared statement and how she was now offering a different account of what had happened. He finished his closing speech by asking why, if the death was the result of an unfortunate accident, she couldn't have given the police a full account at the police station and answered their questions.

Jason Pitter was to have the final word in Teresa's defence before the jury were sent to consider their verdict. In the face of the prosecution evidence, he had to rely heavily on circumstantial and character evidence. He said Teresa and Paul had a good relationship, had enjoyed a happy Christmas together, and were in a good mood before the incident. They had ordered a new car and booked a summer holiday, and were looking forward to the future together. Their occasional arguments were usually about Paul's drinking, but Teresa was used to his challenging behaviour and had learned how to deal with it. She had twice nursed him back to health after his accident and assault, and had absolutely no reason to want to harm him, let alone kill him. The incident was a complete accident that had occurred after Paul had approached Teresa, shouting and swearing, and she had simply pushed him away to get him "out of [her] face", forgetting that she had a knife in her hand – and yes, she *was* angry with him because of the way he was behaving. After learning that her husband had died and being arrested for murder, she was, understandably, shocked and distressed, so couldn't think straight. She relied on her legal adviser and merely followed her advice by not answering police questions.

After lunch, Judge Thackray gave his summing up, which lasted around twenty minutes and was a condensed version of all the evidence we had heard. He ended by asking the question: "Was it a tragic accident or a tragic homicide? If it was homicide, was it murder or manslaughter?" He then gave the jury a 'route to verdict', which was a kind of verbal flow chart he set out, as follows:

1.   Was the stabbing deliberate? If not, Teresa Hanson is not guilty of any offence.
2.   If the stabbing was deliberate, are you sure that the defendant intended to cause *serious* harm? If you are sure, you must find the defendant guilty of murder.
3.   If she didn't intend to cause serious harm, did she intend to cause *some* harm? If yes, she is guilty of

manslaughter. If no, she is not guilty of murder or manslaughter.

Judge Thackray then reminded them that the appointed foreperson must chair the discussions, act as spokesperson, and deliver the verdict. He required a unanimous decision from the twelve jurors.

The jury then retired to consider their verdict. They'd had their legal guidance from the judge; it was now their job to decide on the facts. I wondered what they were all thinking. Did they, like me, still have unanswered questions? I imagined that many of the points that had troubled me would also cause them concern. Would they be influenced by the emotion of the whole disastrous episode and its devastating effects on the family? Could they bring themselves to believe that a loving middle-aged mother and grandmother of good character, whom so many people eulogised, was in fact a murderer? How would they cope with the responsibility of deciding the fate of this seemingly harmless woman? All eyes were on them as they filed out of the court into the jury room to begin their deliberations.

What followed was a state of limbo. Nobody knows whether a jury will take two hours or two days to come to a decision. The jury delivering their verdict is the culmination of the whole process, and is normally the most dramatic part of the trial. Nobody wants to miss it. The tension for the family must have been unbearable. The reporters didn't want to miss it, but couldn't afford to sit around waiting. I decided that after all this time, I wasn't going to risk missing it, even though they might not reach a decision by the end of the day.

This was my fifth full day at the court, and I had by now become very familiar with the facilities, and regularly made use of them. The coffee machine was, inconveniently, located on the ground floor, but the coffee was reasonably priced at £1 a cup. As the weather was usually warm, I made frequent use of the water fountain situated near to the court, even though it was constantly running out of paper cups. I kept having to go and ask for more, as nobody seemed to replenish them. In the end I gave up and started bringing my own drinks, but that caused hold-ups at security when entering the building. There was also a vending machine near the water fountain, which sold bottled drinks and snacks such as crisps and chocolate bars. You could purchase a Mars bar, a Double Decker or a Twix. I guess there were quite a few people looking for a Fudge. This machine was used frequently, because nobody wanted to leave the building in case they missed something – or maybe it was just out of boredom. Either way, it wasn't great for my diet.

I managed to keep myself busy by writing notes, by doing research on my phone, and occasionally by chatting with somebody. On one of my visits to the gents' toilets, I had another strange encounter. When I entered, the place seemed empty, but I was conscious of having been followed in. It wasn't anybody I recognised. I don't remember seeing him in court, although it is possible that he visited without me noticing. One of the unwritten rules when using public toilets is that you don't speak to strangers. This guy clearly didn't understand the rules. After I'd done the necessary and walked to the handbasin to wash my hands, he said, "I don't think she's guilty of murder, do you? Manslaughter at best."

I looked up at him to check again whether I knew him, but I still didn't recognise him. I said, "I don't think we are supposed to discuss it." I'm sure it sounded rather blunt and a bit pompous, but I was caught off guard. I then walked out thinking, If I don't know him, he probably has no idea who I am either. I still don't remember seeing him before, and I never saw him again.

I reflected on this brief interaction and wondered if I had been set up. Had he been sent, officially or unofficially, to try to find out what I was up to? Was he a friend of the family? I'd had similar experiences when I was a police officer, in which I'd believed that I'd had encounters with so-called 'integrity testers' to root out dishonest or corrupt officers. Or maybe I was getting a bit paranoid and all this waiting around was starting to get to me.

The day ended with everybody being called back into the courtroom at 4pm. The jury entered and took their seats. The judge asked the appointed foreman if they had reached a verdict upon which they all agreed. After the foreman replied in the negative, the judge asked the jury to return at 9.30am to continue their deliberations, and the court was adjourned until the next day. It felt like a waste of two hours. Nobody had really expected a verdict today, but they'd been afraid to leave early. At least I could go home now and return tomorrow, when the jury would have the whole day to consider the outcome.

Wednesday 21 June

The court reassembled at 10am, the judge entered, and as usual we were instructed to "all rise". The jury were then shown in, and Judge Thackray went through the formality of confirming that they were still deliberating, and reaffirmed that a unanimous verdict was required. The jury then departed to resume their discussions, and we exited the court once again.

By now I had learned to pass the time by writing notes, chatting to reporters, and looking up relevant information on the Internet via my smartphone. Occasionally I went for a walk within the building to stretch my legs and maybe get a coffee. All the while, I was conscious of avoiding the family and respecting them at this crucial stage. It felt rather like waiting in the A&E department at the hospital.

We were called in just before 12pm to be informed that the jury were no nearer a decision and that the court would adjourn for lunch. I was hungry and desperately needed some fresh air and exercise, so took a walk into Hull's Old Town and treated myself to a plate of fish and chips. I returned after lunch for another long wait, until we were called back into court in the early afternoon. I felt quite excited. Was this it? Unfortunately not. The jury confirmed that they were no nearer reaching a verdict, and in light of this Judge Thackray adjourned proceedings for the day and we all got an early finish. I believe one of the barristers had an appointment elsewhere. After checking the availability of members of the jury, the judge decided on an early start at 8.30am the following day and advised them to bring a packed lunch. It sounded as if he was expecting a long day.

Thursday 22 June

It was an early start, and this was the day when everybody was expecting a verdict. This case would finally come to a conclusion. It had been hampered by all kinds of problems and had overrun by four days, causing even more difficulties. Nevertheless, we had a whole day ahead of us, and I was fascinated to hear the outcome. As for the judge, the barristers and the court staff, I got the impression that they just wanted the case settled and out of the way, as it had clearly caused so many logistical problems. As expected, there was more than the usual trickle of reporters, as they too were anticipating a dramatic conclusion.

We all entered Court One just after 8.30am and, after the formalities were completed, the foreman of the jury said he had two questions for the judge. On behalf of the jury, first of all he wanted to know if a verdict of involuntary manslaughter was open to them. Second, they requested a copy of the pathologist's report.

Judge Thackray seemed taken aback. To the first question he simply said "No," and seemed slightly exasperated, as though he was thinking, You couldn't have been listening when I was giving my legal directions. He seemed more sympathetic to the second question, and informed the jury: "Unfortunately, the rules don't allow it, but I can read out any part of it." This wasn't followed up. Sensing a bit of a stalemate, the judge went on to advise them that he would like a unanimous verdict and would like them to aim for this.

However, if it became obvious that this was not possible, he would accept a majority verdict of eleven to one or even ten to two.

Involuntary manslaughter is when (a) the death of a person occurs following an unlawful act which is seen as dangerous, but the act is undertaken with no intention to kill or seriously harm anybody and is one step removed from the consequences (such as setting fire to a building, not realising that it is occupied), or (b) the death is caused through gross negligence. Judge Thackray had already directed that if the jury considered the stabbing to have been unintentional, Teresa should be acquitted. If, however, they considered the act to be deliberate, it could only be deemed manslaughter (instead of murder) if they believed that she had no intention of causing at least really serious harm. With that, the court was cleared once again and the jurors returned to their discussions.

What happens in a jury room is private, and should always remain so. However, on occasions you get a little bit of an insight into which way the wind is blowing. This was just such an occasion. The jury had enquired about a verdict of involuntary manslaughter, which was obviously under consideration. We also knew that they couldn't all agree – hence the judge's offer to accept a majority verdict. This told us that in all likelihood, half the jury believed it was manslaughter and the other half that it was either murder or an accident. But these are guesses – only twelve people know the truth.

We were called back into court before lunch, and it was clear that some behind-the-scenes discussions had taken place. It was likely that the jury usher had given the judge a progress update. The judge officially asked the foreman of the jury if there was any realistic prospect of reaching a majority verdict. The head of the jury replied "No", and Judge Thackray formally discharged them from their duties. They needn't have brought their packed lunches after all.

So, after a trial lasting nearly eight days and the jury deliberating for about eleven hours, it was stalemate and we still didn't have a verdict. There was no obvious reaction from the family, and Teresa looked confused. I guessed that they were all wondering what would happen next. Maybe they hoped that the prosecution wouldn't seek a retrial, she would walk free, and the whole nightmare would be over. I felt an enormous sense of anticlimax. I'd spent seven days attending, researching and writing, with lots of (im)patient waiting around. Had it all been for nothing? Had my opportunity to write a book just disappeared? Even a retrial would mean that the work I'd done so far would be rendered obsolete.

Alistair MacDonald stood up and soon put an end to the doubt. He said he would be seeking a retrial at the earliest opportunity. The judge said he would like all the legal staff involved in this trial to be available for the next one. I suppose it made sense, as everybody was now very familiar with the case, which would avoid the prospect of somebody new having to get up to speed with everything that had gone before and preparing for the new trial. After checking their diaries and hastily rearranging some appointments, the judge and both barristers came up with a date for the retrial. It would begin on Monday 11 September 2023, and was once again optimistically scheduled for five days. This was nearly three months away, and I had no idea if I would be available. The family must have been wondering if this ordeal would ever end. They would have to go through it all again, but maybe the hung jury gave them cause for hope. Teresa was told that, as usual, she would have to remain on the premises for an extra half-hour to give the jury time to depart. I imagined she would be spending time with her defence counsel, discussing what it all meant. After that, she was free to leave, with the same bail conditions as before. These included not discussing the case with anybody. The family had sat through the whole trial, listening to all the evidence. Some had served as witnesses, and Teresa's son, Ryan, had been a prosecution witness. How common is it for a defendant to be allowed to associate freely with a prosecution witness? I wondered if this bail condition was realistic and how it could possibly be enforced.

The reporters dispersed to write their copy or prepare for their television news bulletin. I imagine they write most of it in advance and prepare for a variety of alternative outcomes such as 'guilty of murder', 'guilty of manslaughter' and 'acquitted'. I'm sure they leave space for the reaction of the defendant and their family and any comments from the judge. I wondered if they had prepared 'hung jury' reports. If not, they were going to be busy rewriting their drafts.

I left the court feeling a bit deflated, as if I had read a book right up to the last chapter, then left it on the bus and never found out how the story ended. The judge and the barristers must have been holding their heads in their hands, at least metaphorically. The frustration of the numerous delays, the rearranging of appointments and the shuffling of work commitments to accommodate this trial had all been in vain. They would have to do it all again from the beginning.

When I got home, I checked my diary for the week commencing 11 September and found that it was blank. At the end of the following week I was going away with my wife for our anniversary. We had tickets to see the rock singer Suzi Quatro. (Younger readers may have to do an Internet search.) This gave me a lift, as I knew I could attend the retrial. The case was again scheduled for five days so, even allowing for the inevitable delays, I thought it unlikely it could last more than two weeks. I then started thinking of the positives. I began to view what had happened as a kind of dress rehearsal and practice for the real thing. This time I would know what to expect, and I would take more notes and be better prepared.

18

The Retrial

Monday 11 September

During the original trial, the weather had been mainly fine and I had dressed mostly in short sleeves, which was not only more comfortable but made things easier when going through security. Now, as well as being a bit cooler, the weather was wet and windy. I found myself a different car park in which to leave my car. Apart from being under cover, it was the type that recorded your entrance time, and you paid only for the time you were there. Previously I had parked in a pay and display car park, where you had to guess how long you would be staying, which was a risky business. I usually paid for a few hours until lunchtime and then popped out during the break to get some lunch and buy another parking ticket.

This time round, I was better prepared. With the unpredictable weather, I thought I'd need a coat and an umbrella. Having found the new car park, I thought it wouldn't be necessary to go out at lunchtime at all, so it would save time and hassle if I took a sandwich and thereby reduced my expenditure on both lunch and parking. As I set off on that first morning, I felt as if I were starting a new term at school following the long holiday. I even had a new bag, containing my packed lunch, my notepads and pens (always have a spare pen) and my compact umbrella. The only things I lacked were a ruler, a protractor and a pencil case.

I walked from my car through the drizzle and arrived at the court in plenty of time. It was just as well. At security I was required to empty my bag, have a drink from my water bottle, and have my umbrella closely examined in case it doubled as a weapon of some sort. This was in addition to the usual ritual of removing my belt, watch and jewellery and being scanned. My lunch also got a quick once-over and I joked, "Cheese and tomato today." Not a flicker. To be fair, I'm sure the security staff had heard it all before, and so they exercised their right to silence.

Once I'd got dressed again and repacked my bag, I went up the stairs to a fairly empty concourse. It felt as if I'd moved up a year at school, because I was now familiar with the building and the routine, and I confess to feeling a little bit smug as I watched others struggling to find their way around. I checked which court we were in, and was pleased to find that we were in the familiar surroundings of Court One. I took my seat on the concourse away from Court One and waited for everybody else to arrive. The family all arrived together, including Teresa herself, and took their seats close to the entrance to the appointed court. I didn't want to get off on the wrong foot again, so did my best to ignore them until I caught a glimpse of them nudging each other and pointing in my direction. They must have hoped that I was just another bad memory, and must now be thinking, Oh no, he's here again. I don't remember seeing any reporters, so I presume they thought today would be a day of formalities and not worth attending for.

At exactly 10am an usher emerged and announced, in the familiar booming voice: "The case of Teresa Hanson."

There was definitely a feeling of déjà vu as the family filed into the court and Teresa took her customary position in the defendant's partitioned section of the court that used to be called 'the dock'. I followed at a respectful distance, and entered the court to find that all of the front row seats of the public gallery were occupied by the family. I took my usual seat towards the back. The cast was the same as before: the judge, the advocates, the clerk and even the ushers. It definitely felt a little bit like *Groundhog Day*.

After the initial formalities had been completed, the first person to speak was Jason Pitter, the defence barrister representing Teresa. Out of the blue, he stood up and said to Judge Thackray that his client was prepared to plead guilty to a charge of manslaughter. I was so shocked I actually wondered if I'd heard him correctly. I wished there was someone with me who could have confirmed what I thought he'd said. I looked round to see other people's reactions. Everybody seemed unmoved. It later transpired that Teresa had made the same offer at the original trial. That must have been the day I was absent, which would explain why I was the only one surprised by the news. The judge responded by saying that it was up to the prosecution.

The prosecuting barrister, Alistair MacDonald, then rose to his feet to say that there was "no basis" for accepting a charge of manslaughter, and made reference to the previous trial. I interpreted this as his way of saying that Teresa couldn't have it both ways: she couldn't, on the one hand, claim (on oath) that Paul's death was an accident, but then offer a guilty plea for manslaughter which would require her to admit to deliberately stabbing him.

Judge Thackray then commented that "Mr Pitter could alter his position – I have no problem either way." I assumed that was code to tell Mr Pitter that his client would need to change her evidence in order for the prosecution to accept the plea. That would be an interesting turn of events. After vigorously claiming at the original trial that it was a pure accident, she would now have to admit that it was, in fact, deliberate. Given that her evidence had been given on oath, wouldn't that amount to an admission of perjury?

Mr MacDonald then responded by saying, "I have my instructions and the trial must go ahead." This seemed to be said through gritted teeth. It was as though he wanted to say, 'It would be a sensible way of resolving this case, but my paymasters, the Crown

Prosecution Service, insist she is tried for murder.' I can understand the CPS pushing for a murder conviction, given the strength of the evidence – especially because the deliberate act/accident issue was such a huge stumbling block. Unless Teresa changed her evidence, as Mr MacDonald himself had said, there was no basis for a charge of manslaughter. She had never been charged with manslaughter so, as it stood, only a jury could find her guilty of this offence as an alternative to murder. The trial, on a charge of murder, would go ahead.

Shortly afterwards there was an adjournment, as apparently the files had been delayed. I am not sure who was responsible for bringing the files into court, but there were some serious traffic delays that morning. This trial seemed to be cursed. We retook our seats on the concourse, and I then saw the two police officers attached to the case hurrying past carrying two large boxes of files. They looked slightly stressed as they bustled into the courtroom to liaise with the prosecutors. There was then a further delay while they sorted themselves out and prepared to begin the trial.

19

The New Jury

At 10.50am we were called back into court, and I was able to witness the jury being sworn in. It was quite a bizarre spectacle as approximately twenty ordinary men and women stood round the perimeter of the courtroom, looking very uncomfortable and out of place. One by one, the clerk of the court picked out the names of the selected jurors, who then took their places in their allocated seats on the jurors' bench. It reminded me of a budget version of a reality television game show. The eight or so candidates who weren't selected were then escorted out of the courtroom. I'm not sure who could be judged the winners – the twelve who were selected or the eight who weren't. Each of the twelve then confirmed their identity and took the oath or affirmation: "I swear by Almighty God [or I do solemnly, sincerely and truly declare and affirm] that I will faithfully try the defendant and give a true verdict according to the evidence."

The seven men and five women who had been randomly selected looked very apprehensive as they settled in their places and were addressed by Judge Thackray. They each had a large ring binder file in front of them, and the judge informed them that it was their personal file for the duration of the trial, but that it must not be removed from the building. The file had subject dividers which split the guidance and evidence packs into different sections. These contained information on jurors' responsibilities, court etiquette, law and procedure. The evidence was made up of reports, transcripts, photographs, plans and diagrams, which were numbered to correspond with whoever was testifying at the time. They too must have felt a bit like their first day at a new school. They were told they were free to make notes in the files.

The judge then gave the jury a 'pep talk' about how important their role was, and thanked them for their time. He was quite open about the fact that this was a retrial, and said that their first duty was to appoint a foreperson to act as the chair and spokesperson. The induction became more serious when he warned them not to do any of their own research into the case, including Internet searches, and not to do any of their own investigations, such as visiting the scene. This probably served to plant the idea into their heads, especially as a mountain of information was available online following the original trial in June. He then instructed them not to discuss the case with anybody other than fellow jurors, and only then when all twelve were present. He finished by warning that not adhering to these instructions could be seen as a contempt of court. I wondered how on earth this could possibly be monitored and enforced.

Judge Thackray then prepared the members of the jury for what was to come. He told them that this was a "tragic case" wherein a couple had previously enjoyed a long and happy marriage, and warned them not to be influenced by the emotion of it all. I wrote down my thoughts at this stage:

Surely by labelling it as a "tragic case" Judge Thackray is already influencing the jury's emotions? You could argue that every case which involves the loss of an innocent life is tragic. Second, telling the jury that the Hansons enjoyed a long and happy marriage is just an opinion. After thirty-three years it was indeed a long marriage, but was it really happy? Teresa herself has said that she endured many years of verbal and mental abuse. Their neighbours heard loud and tempestuous arguments through the wall of their

*adjoining house. As this is not a point of law, I would have
thought the question of whether or not the marriage was
a happy one is a fact for the jury to decide based on the
evidence, not on the judge's opinion.*

It was now 11.10am and, astonishingly, the trial was adjourned
until the next morning. I presume this was because the judge or one
of the barristers had other business to attend to – in which case,
why was it necessary to delay proceedings until the prosecution files
arrived? No evidence had been given. The trial wasn't even under
way. So after only thirty minutes of administrative tasks and forty
minutes of delays, and only seventy minutes after first being called
into court, we were on our way home. At the first trial, I had been
disappointed to miss the first day. It now seemed like a blessing.

20

The Prosecution Case II

Tuesday 12 September

Day two of the retrial began at 10.15am with Alistair MacDonald outlining the case for the prosecution. This was an overview of the evidence the jury would be hearing over the next day or two, presented on behalf of the Crown, which they believed would prove "beyond reasonable doubt" that Teresa Hanson was guilty of murder. As you might expect, it was a 'carbon copy' of the address he gave in the first trial. I would imagine he had retained his original notes and used them once again, as nothing had changed since June. As a quick reminder, he went through the details of the following:

- the events of 28 December 2022
- the 999 calls
- the ambulance's role
- the original arrest by police for grievous bodily harm, and Teresa's 'significant statement'
- the news of Paul's death
- Teresa's arrest for murder
- the police interviews and Teresa's prepared statement
- the evidence of the forensic pathologist
- the evidence of the forensic scientist
- the evidence from Teresa and Paul's son.

At 11.15am there was a break halfway through the prosecution's overview to allow Mr MacDonald time to liaise with the forensic pathologist, Dr Michael Parsons, who had now arrived at court and was preparing to give his testimony. After half an hour Mr MacDonald resumed and completed his address to the jury before reading out the written statements. These were from witnesses whose evidence had been accepted and was therefore uncontested by the defence.

All this was a lot to take in for the newly sworn-in jury, particularly as it wasn't always in chronological order. All of the uncontested statements were read out first, followed by the live witness testimony, so there was a lot of toing and froing with dates and incidents. I sometimes found it confusing, and I was hearing it for the second time.

All the statements had been read out by 1.05pm, and we were ready to go on to hear the live witness evidence. This seemed late for a lunch break, but I suspect it had been designed to give Dr Parsons plenty of time to prepare his evidence, as he had travelled some distance to be there. I was feeling hungry by this time and was glad I didn't have to go out and purchase another pay and display ticket for the car park as I had done previously. I would more than likely have had a penalty charge notice put on my car by now if I'd followed the old routine. Instead, I was glad I could remain inside and enjoy my packed lunch without going outside into the wind and rain and going through the security searches again on my return. I used the time to catch up on my notes and observe what else was going on around me.

Dr Michael Parsons

We were called back into court at 2.15pm, and Dr Parsons was immediately called into the witness box to take the oath. After introducing himself and outlining his qualifications and experience, he was once again led through his evidence in chief by Alistair

MacDonald. In his softly spoken voice, Dr Parsons told the jury that he had examined the body of Paul Hanson during the post-mortem at Hull Royal Infirmary. He explained that the death was caused by a single stab wound to the chest, 129 centimetres (four feet three inches) from the heel of Paul's foot. Using a lot of medical jargon and then translating it into layperson's terms, he described in great detail the sequence of events which had caused Paul's heart to stop beating, which led to his death. He talked about the amount of force that would be required to cause this type of injury, and quoted research into 'accidental stabbings' from America and Australia. In his expert opinion, although the theoretical possibility of this type of accidental stabbing could not be ruled out, it was "highly unlikely" that Paul had walked onto a lightly gripped knife. Finally, he spoke about the actions of somebody trying to push another person away, suggesting that the flat of the hand would most likely be used. He questioned how somebody holding a knife could push somebody away and manage to stab them with the necessary force to seriously injure them.

It is worth noting that the defence team had commissioned a second post-mortem on Paul's body; this practice is, I believe, fairly routine. The defence pathologist was not called as a witness, so we can assume that their findings weren't significantly different from those of Dr Parsons. It is probably because of this that the cross-examination by Jason Pitter was brief and uncontroversial. Mr Pitter's line of questioning centred mainly on Dr Parsons' assertion with regard to the practicalities of pushing another person with the flat of one's hand and on his conclusions about the pattern of bloodstains. Dr Parsons conceded that these matters were outside his area of expertise and his opinions were offered as a layperson. There was a brief re-examination by Mr MacDonald to clarify some of Dr Parsons' answers, and he concluded his evidence at 3.45pm.

This seemed an appropriate time to finish, as we'd had a full day of listening to evidence and it was a lot for the jury to take in.

It was also too late for the next witness, Ryan Hanson, to begin giving evidence and be cross-examined. The judge was clearly of the same mind, and he formally adjourned proceedings until 10am the following day.

21

Another Strange Turn of Events

Wednesday 13 September

I attended the court on day three with a bit more optimism. The trial was now well under way and on schedule to finish by the end of the week. I was looking forward to the prosecution completing their evidence, and there was a possibility that the defence would begin their case before the day was out. That, of course, would mean Teresa entering the witness box, although I was sure Jason Pitter would try to avoid that happening, as they would prefer to start their defence on a new day. I should have known better…

After a bit of waiting around, we all entered the court at 10.20am and took our customary positions in the public gallery. The judge entered the courtroom to the now-routine instruction: "All rise." There seemed to be a bit of scurrying around. I was waiting for the jury to be shown in, but they never arrived. What appeared to be frantic discussions were taking place between the clerk of the court and the judge. The two barristers looked as confused as I was, wondering what was going on. Teresa was at the back of the court, looking rather bemused. It was obvious that something out of the ordinary was happening.

We had barely taken our seats when Judge Thackray, with a face like thunder, announced rather abruptly that he had "urgent business" to deal with, and promptly rose to his feet and left. There was a shocked silence, and everyone was looking at each other, just stopping short of shrugging their shoulders. People were metaphorically scratching their heads and began whispering to each other, no doubt speculating as to the cause of the judge's sudden departure. Three or four reporters discussing the matter on the press bench were probably sharing theories as to what might be happening.

The general hubbub became gradually louder, as it might when a teacher leaves a classroom and nobody is left in charge. The clerk of the court suddenly announced in a raised voice (which was by now necessary to be heard above the ambient buzz), "Court as chambers," and then asked everybody to leave the courtroom. 'Court as chambers' is a legal phrase meaning that the judge and the prosecution and defence teams have urgent business to discuss in the absence of not only the jury but also the press and the public. They usually dispense with their wigs and other regalia, and it becomes more of a meeting than a formal procedure. In the past they would meet in the judge's chambers (his office), but I think it's sometimes more convenient to clear the court – hence the phrase 'court as chambers'.

We all eventually left the courtroom, but there was a distinct reluctance, as I think people felt they were owed at least some explanation as to what was going on. The reporters remained seated and continued chatting among themselves. The family left as a group, followed by the police, and Teresa was escorted out of a side door. The barristers and ushers had also vacated the room, and the court was now virtually empty. I picked up my things and decamped to the concourse, hoping to be given an update. The reporters were the last to leave, and they came out and sat on the seats behind me. I couldn't relax in case I missed something. I didn't even visit the coffee machine, fearing that I might be absent just when there was a dramatic development. Instead, I continually scanned the concourse for any hints or clues.

After about forty-five minutes, Mr Pitter emerged in the company of Teresa, and the two of them, along with other members of their team, entered a vacant consultation room and closed the door behind them. I could hear some of the conversations between the journalists behind me. Speculation was now at fever pitch. Had the defendant decided she could not go through the ordeal of giving evidence and being cross-examined a second time? Had she decided to change her plea to guilty? Her offer to plead guilty to manslaughter had already been rejected, so had she decided to cut her losses and plead guilty to murder in exchange for a lighter minimum sentence? Had the prosecution and the defence come to an arrangement and cut a deal? Had some conclusive evidence suddenly come to light which would prove Teresa's guilt or secure an acquittal? Nobody knew for sure, but we couldn't help speculating.

After a while, Mr Pitter and his team emerged from the consultation room with Teresa, who then joined her family sitting in the concourse. I, along with everybody else, couldn't help watching the family's reaction for any pointers. I put on my glasses and observed their body language and facial expressions. I was too far away to hear any of their conversation or even to attempt lip-reading. Once they had been made aware of the situation, it was noticeable that they became more relaxed and even began smiling. Whatever had happened seemed to have been to their advantage.

After two hours of waiting, we were all put out of our misery when we were called back into court at 12.40pm. Once everybody had taken their seat, Judge Thackray entered the court and made a short and slightly cryptic speech. He said in a very solemn voice that there had been "a problem" with the jury which he had been unable to resolve, and therefore he had taken the decision to dismiss the jury and abort the trial. This was greeted with stunned silence by those who weren't already aware. The judge then said, rather matter-of-factly, that the court was adjourned for the day and proceedings would recommence at 10am tomorrow. In the meantime, these events should not be reported on.

My date with Suzi Quatro was now in real jeopardy.

Thursday 14 September

I arrived at court early and deliberately sat close to the reporters to see if they had further information on the previous day's events. I got talking to one of the television reporters, who told me that he had put a note in to the judge asking how he should report the fact that the trial had been aborted. He had been giving nightly bulletins on the progress of the case, and now had the problem of reporting the same evidence from two days ago without an explanation as to why. Alternatively, he could stop reporting for a couple of days and then resume his evening updates where he'd left off. Another newspaper journalist had been told that the trial had been stopped because two members of the jury had been seen talking to the defendant's family. There was no indication as to who had initiated the contact. Did the family approach the jurors or was it vice versa? Obviously, the journalist wouldn't reveal his source, and there was no way this could be verified.

At 10.20am the press were called into court for a briefing with Judge Thackray. I believe this was to make it clear that he had issued reporting restrictions and, so as not to prejudice the hearing, the press were forbidden to mention the termination of the previous trial.

I have since contacted the court who informed me this matter can now be reported as a 'jury irregularity'.

22

Trial Number Three

Here we go again. At 10.40am, the usher gave the familiar cry: "The case of Teresa Hanson." After taking our seats in the court and then rising to our feet for the judge's entrance, there were some brief discussions between the judge and the barristers. I can't be certain, but I thought I heard Judge Thackray mention contempt of court, stating that he didn't intend to initiate proceedings on this occasion. I checked to see if there were any absentees from the family group, but they all seemed to be present. From this I made the assumption that, if the story was true, the family had been the innocent parties in the unfortunate interaction with the former jury members. I can't imagine them being allowed to remain in the court if they were in any way culpable. On the other hand, you might ask yourself why the family were smiling on being told the news. Could it be because the judge had decided to take no further action? Either way, I wondered why the individuals concerned weren't subject to contempt of court proceedings as Judge Thackray had threatened. With the retrial now running way behind schedule, perhaps he had enough on his plate and didn't want to draw attention to this latest fiasco. Maybe, if the family *were* responsible, he thought they'd suffered enough. And were the reporting restrictions solely in the interest of justice? Were the principles of open justice a little bit compromised? I don't know.

I was surprised to find that the *new* new jury had already been sworn in and shown to their seats, having, presumably, also been given their formal instructions by the judge. There was a definite feeling of rushing things through to make up for lost time. On this occasion, there were six men and six women. This is one of the facts that reporters love to mention at the beginning of a trial. I wondered if they would report it this time, having already stated that the previous jury was made up of seven men and five women. That would be quite difficult to explain. Would anyone actually notice?

With a renewed sense of urgency, Alistair MacDonald once again began outlining the prosecution case. I bet he was glad he'd held on to all of his notes from the original trial as he went through the case in detail for the third time of asking.

At 11.20am, when Mr MacDonald was about halfway through his address, proceedings were suddenly halted as a member of the jury seemed to be trying to attract the judge's attention. The usher went over to see what the problem was and was given a note by the juror, which was passed to the judge. There was a palpable feeling of frustration in the court as you could almost hear everybody thinking, What now? After reading the note, Judge Thackray invited the jury to take a short break and shared the contents of the note, which said that Juror Number Nine, who was following the evidence in her guidebook during Mr MacDonald's address, had found some handwritten notes from a previous juror in relation to the previous (aborted) trial. He didn't reveal what the notes referred to. Oh dear. It would seem that the court staff, in their haste to get things moving as quickly as possible, had forgotten to check or renew the jurors' guidebooks. Judge Thackray announced that he wished to discuss the matter with "counsel in chambers", which is a legal term for 'we need a private meeting in my office'. So once again we were all asked to vacate the courtroom and take a short break. The whole trial seemed to be descending into farce.

About fifteen minutes later, we were recalled into court to hear the judge announce that the notes were not prejudicial, Juror Number Nine had not read them, and the trial could proceed. How convenient. I would love to have been a fly on the wall in the judge's chambers when they were deciding what to do next. I knew they were always going to find a way round it, as surely they couldn't possibly discharge the jury and start a fourth trial? In any case, I doubt there would have been sufficient jurors; this case alone would have burned through thirty-six jurors in four days. In an attempt to make light of it, Judge Thackray said, "It never rains, but it pours."

The jury were all sent out again for a 'coffee and convenience' break. I suspect this was more for the convenience of the court staff than the jury, as they now had to go through all the jurors' guidebooks to make sure there were no other notes written in that book or in any of the others. I wouldn't like to have been in the shoes of the individual whose responsibility it had been to check or change the books after the previous trial. After the jury had left, the rest of the court exited and took their seats on the concourse. I sat near to the reporters, and among them there was a sense of utter incredulity. As one of the newspaper journalists said, "This is becoming the story." And it would have been, except for the fact that Judge Thackray had once again restricted their reporting of it. That possibly had more to do with covering up the court's embarrassment than prejudicing the trial. Maybe justice isn't as open as we are led to believe. Following the completion of the trial, the reporting restrictions have now been lifted.

I then looked across to the next row of seats to see the forlorn figure of Dr Michael Parsons, the forensic pathologist who for the third time had been called back from his base in Royal Leamington Spa (about 140 miles away) to give his evidence. I can imagine the profuse apologies when informing him of the need to return only two days after last giving his evidence. I would guess he had had a very early start in order to arrive mid-morning, when he would have been expecting to give his evidence, only to find that there had been further delays and he wouldn't now be required until the afternoon.

This would mean a very long day for him, but – as was so often the case – the taxpayer would pick up the bill.

The short coffee break turned out to be a long coffee break, and we were called to return at 12.40pm. Judge Thackray apologised and said that the reason for the further delay was that one of the jury members had been "struggling with their emotions" but that it had now been resolved. Although sympathetic with the juror concerned, I think we were all struggling with our emotions. They were still on their first day. For the rest of us, this was our twelfth or thirteenth day in total.

Without any further drama, Mr MacDonald completed his outlining of the prosecution evidence, and then we all took a delayed and shortened lunch break. We returned at 2pm to find that Court One had been commandeered by another trial. Apparently, this was to accommodate their need for the extra technical facilities available there. I am guessing that this was the video technology through which cases are often heard remotely – to save the need for the defendant to leave prison, for example. We had been allocated Court Four, which seemed a bit of a demotion, but when we entered I found it far more spacious. It was configured the opposite way round to Court One, so it was like a mirror image. I took my seat at the back of the public gallery, where I found I was in a more elevated position than before. This time I had to look to my left to witness proceedings, and had a much clearer view of the jury, but from a greater distance.

23

The Evidence of the Forensic Pathologist

At 2.10pm Dr Michael Parsons entered the witness box, and once again he was led through his evidence by Alistair MacDonald. It appeared that the 'batting order' had changed, with the forensic pathologist opening for the prosecution this time. In the original trial, we had heard the seven witness statements followed by the recordings of the 999 calls before any live evidence. I suspected that following the morning's events, there had been a reshuffle to ensure that Dr Parsons gave his evidence today, to avoid asking him to return for a fourth time. I don't think this had much of an effect on the chronology of evidence, but I would imagine that, with the trial now so far behind schedule, it was the least of the judge's worries.

I don't know what they are supposed to look like but, to me, Dr Parsons appeared more like an IT middle manager than a forensic pathologist. Dressed in a light grey Marks & Spencer-type business suit, he once again spoke assuredly, directing his responses to the jury in his quiet but confident voice. After going through the formalities of taking the oath, introducing himself and listing his professional qualifications, Dr Parsons gave his evidence in chief.

He told the court that he had thoroughly examined the body of the deceased, Paul Hanson, in the course of a post-mortem carried out at Hull Royal Infirmary. He stated that he could not find any "defensive injuries" on Paul's hands or arms. We were informed that Paul was 167 centimetres (five feet six inches) tall

122

and weighed ninety-four kilograms (fourteen stone eleven pounds). Dr Parsons had taken a blood sample and found that it contained 125 milligrams of alcohol per 100 millilitres of blood. The drink-drive limit in England is eighty milligrams, so Paul was over 50% above what is deemed safe to be in control of a vehicle. This would be sufficient to cause a change of behaviour in the average social drinker. (The drink-drive limit is thought to be roughly equal to four units of alcohol, so Paul's reading would equate to approximately six or seven units, or three large glasses of red wine. This is consistent with Teresa's evidence.) From his examination, Dr Parsons was able to confirm that Paul's spleen had been removed following the car accident in 1997. He explained to the jury that the function of the spleen is to prevent infection, and that following a splenectomy a patient would be more vulnerable to disease. On the skull there was evidence of neurosurgery having taken place following the brain injury sustained in the assault that occurred in 2010. Dr Parsons confirmed that this type of injury can change someone's personality and behaviour.

He then went on to talk about the fatal injury. It was his understanding that the blade which was believed to have caused the injury was 10.6 centimetres (4.2 inches) in length and 1.6 centimetres (0.6 inches) wide. The stab wound was located at nipple height, slightly to the left side of Paul's chest, and measured 8.5 centimetres (3.3 inches) deep and 2.5 centimetres (one inch) wide. Dr Parsons described the wound and compared it to a clock face. He told us that the blade entered Paul's chest at an orientation of two o'clock/eight o'clock and was angled upwards and slightly to the left. After cutting through the clothing, it had entered the body between the fourth and fifth ribs. The knife would have penetrated the skin, fat and muscle before entering and then passing through the heart and out the other side into the aorta, which is the body's main artery. Dr Parsons explained that the pericardial sac surrounds the heart and that its main function is to protect it. In his examination of

Paul's body, he'd found that the sac contained 400 millilitres (0.7 pints) of blood. As the heart beats, the blood is under pressure, so if the heart is penetrated the blood quickly leaks into the pericardial sac. This condition is known as 'cardiac tamponade'. As the sac fills with blood, it restricts the movement of the heart. Dr Parsons told us that the breaching of the heart would have resulted in a loss of integrity and the heart would no longer have been able to pump properly. The blood leaking into the sac would cause a loss of blood volume and, consequently, a loss of pressure. This in turn would cause the heart to beat more rapidly and the arteries to constrict in an effort to compensate and maintain pressure. The body fights a losing battle as the pericardial sac fills with blood and restricts the movement of the heart, until finally it is overwhelmed. Dr Parsons then informed the court that this would cause "profuse bleeding both internally and externally" and, significantly, the "external bleeding would have started rapidly." He ended this section of his testimony by concluding that it was "a sharp force injury produced by a pointed instrument by a thrusting movement".

This is the kind of evidence you normally only hear on a television show such as *Silent Witness*, which is designed to entertain. But this was for real, and the final moments of a much-loved father and grandfather had just been graphically described in a clinical, scientific way. It was fascinating for the neutral observer, but I can't imagine what Paul's family must have been going through, listening to the medical account of the chain of events that had led to his death. There was a very low and sombre mood in the court.

Dr Parsons was then asked by Mr MacDonald what force would have been required to inflict the wound he had just described. Dr Parsons replied that it is a very subjective concept, but a commonly used scale ranges from mild to moderate to severe to extreme. He said that clothing and skin offer the initial protection, but once the skin is penetrated the body offers little resistance unless the knife hits bone or cartilage, which is similar in texture to hard plastic.

He then went on to tell the court that during his examination of the body there was no evidence of any contact with either bone or cartilage. He said that Paul had been wearing a T-shirt and a polo shirt at the time the injury was inflicted. These would have offered minimal resistance to the knife. He therefore concluded that only mild to moderate force would have been required to cause the injuries he had observed.

Mr MacDonald then asked Dr Parsons if, in his expert opinion, the stabbing could have occurred accidentally by Paul walking onto the knife, as Teresa had claimed in her prepared statement. Dr Parsons said that the wound was level with Paul's nipples and 129 centimetres (four feet three inches) from his heel. He understood that Teresa was 155 centimetres (five feet one inch) tall, so this would be approximately shoulder height for her. Most kitchen worktops are ninety centimetres (three feet) from the ground, so there was a difference of approximately thirty-nine centimetres (one foot three inches) from the surface where she had been working to the height of the wound, which was angled upwards and slightly to the left. (Teresa is right-handed, so the angle of the wound is a significant point.) Dr Parsons said he found it "difficult to reconcile the height and angle of the wound with Teresa Hanson's version of events". As we know, Teresa changed her account when her team were required to provide a defence statement: she claimed that, rather than her husband walking onto the knife, she had accidentally stabbed him by pushing him away while chopping onions, forgetting that she was holding the knife.

In response to the question about accidental stabbings generally, Dr Parsons said that the rarity of the scenario "needs to be emphasised". He told the court that there were two pieces of research into this specific subject. The first was carried out in Dallas, Texas in 2001, where 9,562 accidental deaths involving sharp instruments were examined. In most of these cases a drinking glass was responsible for the fatal injury. Only eleven (0.12%) involved stab-like wounds.

Out of these, there was only one case (with supporting evidence) which involved a knife. In this particular instance, the wound had occurred when the victim was attempting to sharpen a knife on a sharpening wheel that had been incorrectly wired. The consequence of this was that the wheel rotated in the opposite direction, causing the knife to travel upwards into the unsuspecting victim's body – clearly, a freak accident. The second piece of research took place in Australia in 2018 and examined 1,136 cases of death caused by a sharp instrument such as a knife. In this study, there were no cases of an accidental single stab wound.

The pathologist concluded his evidence by telling the court that the stab wound was deep and would have required mild to moderate force and the knife to be firmly held. He said that theoretically, a person can run or fall onto a knife, and this possibility couldn't be totally ruled out. But in his expert opinion, it was "highly unlikely" that Paul had walked onto a lightly gripped knife in the way Teresa had described.

Jason Pitter then cross-examined Dr Parsons on behalf of the defence. He questioned him with regard to comments he'd made about the likely pattern of blood on the kitchen floor. Mr Pitter also queried Dr Parsons' answers in relation to the specifics of how the knife would be held while pushing somebody away. In response, Dr Parsons conceded that these were his personal opinions, rather than professional opinions as a forensic pathologist; they weren't in his area of expertise. After a brief re-examination by Mr MacDonald to clarify some of the details, Dr Parsons was allowed to leave the witness box, and he left the court to make the long journey home.

It was now 3.35pm, and Judge Thackray commented on how warm it was in Court Four. He asked, in a rhetorical fashion, if anybody else was feeling uncomfortable with the temperature. Without waiting for a response, he continued: "I'll have the air conditioning looked at." Sensing that the jury had received enough information to consider for one day, he told them they were free to leave and must return at 10am tomorrow. He then formally adjourned proceedings until the following morning, telling Teresa that she must stay in the building until 4.15pm.

The usher went through the closing ritual of "all rise" as the judge hastily departed. I wondered how the conversation would go this evening at the dinner table in the Thackray household. Thursday 14 September had been what you might call 'a bad day at the office'.

24

Catch-Up Day

Friday 15 September

I parked my car in the usual place and took the short walk to the court building. As I approached the corner where the court is situated, I could see a white van parked right in the middle of the court apron. I thought it unusual, as a prison or security van delivering defendants in custody would always enter the secure area at the rear of the building. As I got closer, I could see from the signwriting that the van belonged to an air conditioning company. I had to smile to myself as I walked past because, short of royalty, only a judge could complain about the air conditioning in the afternoon and have someone out fixing it early the next morning. And anybody else foolish enough to park right in front of a court building would more than likely have had their vehicle towed away immediately as a possible terrorist threat. Never underestimate the power of a judge.

Proceedings got under way promptly at 10.04am, with a clear need to make up for lost time. Court Four was now noticeably cooler and less stuffy. On behalf of the prosecution, Alistair MacDonald read out three of the written and agreed statements. These were from the Hansons' next-door neighbours, Rachel and Shaun Trafford, and Michelle Harvey, who was married to Teresa's brother.

As before, the Traffords described their relationships with the Hansons and gave their individual accounts of what they'd heard on the night of 28 December 2022. Most significantly, Shaun said that for ten minutes from about 7.20pm he had heard "banging and slamming of internal doors" coming from the Hansons' adjoining house. He said that this was followed by a period of quiet, which, I would assume, was after the stabbing had occurred and while Teresa was making the emergency call. There was no mention of hearing a dog barking or music being played. After a significant time gap, he witnessed the ambulance arriving. We know that the first 999 call was made at 7.05pm. It seems that the time given by Mr Trafford is inaccurate, as the ambulance arrived at 7.20pm. This statement was taken on the day following the incident (29 December). I can understand why the time of 7.20pm wasn't queried by the statement taker, as it would have been before the details of the paramedic's statement were known. However, once the anomaly was identified (if it ever was), I would have thought that a further statement would have been taken from Mr Trafford to clarify how he had calculated the time. We know that the times given by the paramedic must be accurate, and this is corroborated by the second 999 call, as the ambulance crew arrived while Teresa was still on the telephone. This went on to be significant evidence, and I would have expected the defence team to have highlighted this discrepancy.

Michelle Harvey's statement informed the jury of the Hansons' visit to her house earlier in the day to bring her birthday and Christmas presents. She said that Paul and Teresa were in a good mood, having recently booked a holiday and ordered a new car. They left at about 2.30pm, saying that they were going to Tesco in Goole to get something for their evening meal.

After these statements had been read to the jury, the recordings of the two emergency telephone calls were played to the court once again. These have been documented earlier in this book. Although I had heard the recordings before, they were no less harrowing this time. The jury, of course, would have been hearing them for the first time. I don't know if they had transcripts in their files, but there was a lot of information for them to take in, as the two calls lasted nearly twenty-four minutes in total. On hearing them for the first time, it was difficult not to be affected emotionally. This was not a drama, it was not acting; it was real. When I'd heard the recordings during the original trial, all I could think about was the human tragedy. Two adults had had a relatively trivial argument that had nonetheless ended with one desperately seeking help to save the other's life. The panic, the confusion and the distress were all laid bare for everybody to hear. It must have been hard for the jurors not to let their emotions affect their judgement when analysing the evidential value of what was said in those calls. I know I found it difficult to concentrate and take notes the first time. On this occasion I knew what to expect, so I wasn't as shocked and was able to write down the significant elements. It was still very distressing to listen to the calls for a second time, but taking comprehensive notes enabled me to do a thorough review later on. As had happened the last time they were played, once the recordings had finished there was a stunned silence as everybody tried to process what they'd just heard. The judge deemed this an appropriate time for a break. I looked across at the jury as they filed out of the court in a kind of stupor. I wondered what they were feeling as they went for a well-earned cup of coffee and tried to make sense of it all.

My vigorous note-taking must have caught the attention of Judge Thackray. As soon as the jury had left the courtroom, I saw the clerk of the court walk towards me. He was a tall, slim, bespectacled man in his early thirties, with short brown hair and a single earring. Without introducing himself, he began the conversation with "There's no problem with you doing it, but the judge was wondering why you were taking notes." He said this in quite a loud voice, and members of the Hanson family were still sitting just in front of me.

I felt it was rather inappropriate, as it clearly drew the attention of the remaining family, who were now waiting for my answer. I confess to feeling a little embarrassed, as we were still in an open court. I was tempted to say 'I've actually been doing it all through the trial' or 'If there's no problem with me doing it, why does he need to know?' But I didn't want to upset the judge at this crucial stage of the trial, so I reverted to my usual polite self and said, "Can we discuss this in private, please?"

The clerk then took me into the court foyer and repeated his question, adding, "The judge was wondering what you were writing."

I told him that I merely had an academic interest in the case and was using it as a case study. The reason for my note-taking was that I was considering writing an article or even a book about the trial, although it would probably never happen. I said that now that I was retired, I had nothing better to do. I smiled as I said it, but the clerk didn't see the humour. He thanked me for my honesty and returned to the court to report back to Judge Thackray. I still don't know what prompted this interest. I suspect the judge might have thought I was some kind of rogue journalist. All along I had tried to keep a low profile and go unnoticed, but this was now my fourth encounter with authority figures who seemed obsessed with knowing what I was doing. This was yet another example of open justice being tolerated but, at the same time, regarded with suspicion.

It was now 11.25am, and after the short break Mr MacDonald read out the remaining agreed statements from:

- Andrew Hyland (paramedic)
- PC Adam Lazenby (arresting police officer)
- Dr Paul Stewart (casualty doctor)
- Kathryn Bird (forensic scientist).

As this evidence was in written form, it was exactly the same as in the first trial, and as the content was agreed by the defence, none of the witnesses was made available for cross-examination. I know I've said it before, but this feels wrong. Having already gone through the whole trial back in June, I felt even more uncomfortable hearing what were quite basic statements read out in lieu of live witness testimony.

Nearly all of the statements had been taken shortly after the incident, before further evidence emerged. Quite often statements are rushed and taken in an environment which is far from ideal. As far as I know, none of these witnesses was revisited for a follow-up interview. Second statements can look slightly suspicious, because it can be alleged that they were directed by a police officer who, by then, had the benefit of knowing the bigger picture. But immediately after the incident, nobody knows what is relevant or important. There is a facility for witnesses to be interviewed on video, similarly to a suspect, but the option wasn't considered.

The statements from the neighbours weren't particularly thorough but turned out to be very significant. At the time they were taken, nobody knew what Teresa was going to say in her interview. I believe a more detailed statement from Shaun Trafford about the timings and what he actually heard could have cast doubt on some parts of Teresa's evidence. PC Lazenby's statement was probably written before he went off duty on the same night, because it would be required by the major crime team before interviewing her. A further statement from PC Lazenby, or any other officer who went to the house, could have described the scene in more detail. The paramedics would have disturbed the scene in order to work on Paul; but, knowing that it was a stabbing involving a kitchen knife, more information about the positions of all the kitchen utensils and foodstuffs present might have helped. Photographs taken later are essential, of course, but won't tell you whether there was a smell of onions being cooked or how hot the pan was. The forensic scientist, Kathryn Bird, gave a statement saying that she had examined a black-handled kitchen knife, the measurements of which were consistent with the cuts found on the two bloodstained tops worn by Paul. The knife still had a "distribution of blood and fatty deposits" on its blade. This is the same knife that, we now know, Teresa claimed to have used to chop onions *after* the stabbing. Ms Bird wouldn't have known this at the time of writing her statement. In that statement, there was no mention of any traces of onion on the knife because either it wasn't deemed relevant at the time, or they didn't exist. Either way, it would have been significant evidence which could have been recorded in a follow-up statement and given as live testimony if necessary.

Because these statements lacked detail and were fairly neutral, I am not surprised that they weren't contested. In fact, I would imagine that Jason Pitter was quite relieved. I have summarised the contents of all the written statements earlier in this book.

The reading of the statements was completed by noon, at which time Judge Thackray declared that he would be adjourning the case. This wasn't just for a lunch break, but for the whole weekend. I believe there were availability issues for both the judge and the barristers. He then announced that proceedings would recommence at 10am on *Tuesday*. I imagine they had important appointments on Monday that couldn't be rearranged. After all, the trial had originally been scheduled for five days, so at the time of making subsequent appointments they would have assumed that Teresa's trial would be over by now. Although this is understandable, it is not good for continuity, or for the jury, to have a three-and-a-half-day break in a trial that has only been running for a day and a half.

25

The Completion of the Prosecution Case

Tuesday 19 September

After my unexpectedly long weekend, I returned to Hull Crown Court with my rucksack containing my packed lunch, umbrella, notebook and pen. I arrived at about 9.30am and, after undergoing the security searches, took my seat on the concourse. The family, including Teresa, were already in attendance, sitting close to the entrance of Court Four. They always travelled together and arrived in good time to avoid any risk of encountering members of the jury. I assumed, from where they were sitting, that we had once again been allocated Court Four. There were no reporters in attendance, either because they weren't expecting anything significant to happen that morning or because there were other news stories to cover. I took my seat near to the top of the stairway, close enough to Court Four but at a respectful distance from the family. Being close to the stairs, I could observe people arriving on the concourse and try to work out who each of them was and where they were heading. There was the usual mix of barristers, court officials, security guards, defendants and witnesses. You could always tell the people who weren't employees: apart from not wearing any kind of uniform, they invariably looked uncomfortable and unsure about where to go. A bit like me on my first day on 13 June, which now seemed a long, long time ago.

We had a longer-than-normal wait, and it wasn't until 10.30am that an usher emerged from the entrance to Court Four to make the familiar announcement: "The case of Teresa Hanson."

I took my usual seat: right at the back, with a couple of rows separating me from the family in front. I couldn't help noticing that there was an additional member of the family present. She was a girl who looked to be in her early teens, and the reason I noticed her so quickly was that she kept turning round to look at me as I was writing notes. She would also nudge the person next to her and point straight at me. I put this down to natural curiosity and did my best to ignore it. I wondered if the murder trial of a relative was a suitable event for a child of that age to attend. Unless they are giving evidence, special permission is required for a child under the age of fourteen to sit in the court. I don't know if it had been granted, or perhaps she was over fourteen, but nobody other than me seemed concerned. I then remembered that the children had gone back to school after the summer break more than two weeks ago, so this girl would actually be absent from school. She didn't appear to be ill, so her 'permission for absence' form would have made interesting reading. It later emerged that one of the defence witnesses, Vanessa Lappin, was unwell and couldn't testify in person as she had during the first trial. I wondered if this girl was her daughter and she was unable to take care of her. It is possible that whoever normally looked after the girl in these circumstances had been required at court and so decided to bring her along. It may even have been Teresa herself.

Teresa was sitting at the back of the court, having been shown in by a security guard. I had a better view in Court Four and could see that she was still wearing her wedding ring as well as the ring her son had told the court was made from her husband's ashes. The barristers and officials took their places and we all rose as the judge entered the court.

Ryan Hanson

The next witness for the prosecution was Teresa and Paul's son. You may remember from the first trial that Ryan had given two statements. The first was taken while his mother was still in police custody, and it undermined her prepared statement about being a victim of verbal and mental abuse. This was why he was giving evidence on behalf of the prosecution. The second statement was, I assume, on behalf of the defence. He was, after all, supporting his mother. This statement was more about his parents' relationship, how strong their marriage was, and what good parents and grandparents they were. This was a strange situation, as he would be giving evidence for both the prosecution and the defence. Instead of his evidence in chief, followed by the testing of that evidence by a cross-examination, Ryan's appearance was more like giving evidence in chief twice over: once for the prosecution and once for the defence. Most peculiar.

After being called and entering the witness box, Ryan took the oath once again. As had been the case in the first trial, he was very softly spoken and seemed extremely nervous. As I was sitting right at the back of the room, and as Court Four was much larger than Court One, I found it difficult to hear a lot of what was said. It was almost as if Ryan were deliberately speaking quietly, as though it were a private conversation. It is understandable, and quite natural, to want to speak in hushed tones when discussing intimate matters, such as your parents' relationship, in front of strangers. However, Ryan's testimony was being presented as evidence in a murder trial, and the jury needed to hear it. I don't remember him ever being asked to raise his voice. I would guess that was because his evidence wasn't considered pivotal and the judge didn't want to add to his obvious discomfort. From what I could hear, Ryan gave much the same evidence as in the first trial, which I have summarised earlier in this book.

DC Stuart Quinn

Next up, and concluding the prosecution's evidence, was the officer in the case, DC Quinn. As you would expect, he gave the same evidence as before. I have covered this in a previous chapter, but as a reminder, DC Quinn gave evidence of the following:

- The initial arrest.
- Teresa's arrival at the police station.
- Her subsequent arrest for murder.
- Her lack of injuries.
- The terms of the caution being explained to her, and her confirming that she understood.
- Her representation by an accredited legal representative (not a qualified solicitor).
- Details of her prepared statement, which said, "Over the years, my husband has been verbally and mentally abusive to me. The injury occurred whilst I was holding the knife when he walked onto it. At no time did I intend to kill him or cause him serious harm."
- The interviews in which she gave 'no comment' replies (other than her prepared statement).
- Her being charged with murder at 9.53pm on Friday 30 December 2022 and making no comment in reply.

A brief cross-examination by Jason Pitter merely confirmed some of the details of DC Quinn's evidence.

This marked the end of the case for the prosecution, and I wondered why this time they hadn't played the police bodycam video of the moment Teresa was informed of Paul's death and her subsequent arrest for murder. It may have been to save the defendant, her family and the jury from experiencing the distress of witnessing the horrible spectacle as she was informed that she had not only lost her husband but was now a murder suspect. Maybe the footage was not considered evidentially important and they needed to save some time, even though it was used in the original trial and was only a minute long. Then I remembered why we were in Court Four. It was because we had swapped with a case that needed technical equipment such as video-playing facilities, which I assume Court Four lacked. But surely they couldn't have omitted this piece of evidence just because they were unable to show it on a big screen…could they?

It was 11.40am, and the time seemed right for a break before the defence began their case. I welcomed the break to catch up with my notes and visit the coffee machine on the ground floor. Unfortunately, after I inserted my £1 coin into the slot, the machine informed me that it was out of cups, and I pressed what I thought was the 'coin eject' button to no effect. I looked around for help, or at least to inform somebody, but the only staff on duty seemed to be the security staff at the entrance. I walked towards them before thinking, It's not worth the hassle, and then turned and walked back upstairs without my coffee or my £1 coin.

I took my seat on the concourse and was looking forward to hearing Teresa give her evidence once again. It reminded me of the occasions when I was young and still living with my parents. After a good night out, I would invariably return home several hours late, to be greeted by my angry father standing in the hallway with his hands on his hips. "You've got some explaining to do!" After hearing all the prosecution evidence, I felt Teresa had some explaining to do as well. Except this was serious – *very* serious. Her explanation as to what had happened on the night of 28 December would have to be a lot more convincing than the excuses I gave to my father. Only two people had known the truth of what had actually happened that night, and one of them was, sadly, no longer here. Defendants aren't obliged to give evidence in their own defence, but Teresa was the only real witness for her defence team, and their only hope of an acquittal. In truth, she *had* to give evidence and it had to be convincing. I didn't envy her task.

26

The Case for the Defence II

We were called back into court at 12.05pm and I still hadn't had a coffee. It seemed a strange time for the defence's key witness to begin her evidence – so close to lunchtime. It was obvious that Teresa was going to spend a long time in the witness box, and I don't know if this was deliberate in order to factor in regular breaks or just because they were running late.

Teresa Hanson

Teresa entered the witness box looking quite frail and vulnerable. She was again dressed in her familiar black trouser suit, with her hair down and brushed back over her shoulders. She had already been through this ordeal back in June, and it seemed almost cruel for her to suffer the agony a second time. Perhaps she would find it less strenuous, having already experienced it at her first trial. She would know what to expect even under cross-examination, and so she would, surely, be better prepared. But honestly, I don't believe that anything could have helped to prepare her for what was about to follow: having to explain to a court made up of close relatives and strangers how it came to be that her husband of thirty-three years, the father of her children, had died as a direct result of her actions. She fully accepted that she was responsible for Paul's death, but claimed that it was all a terrible accident. She admitted that she was holding the knife at the time it penetrated his heart, but denied that she had intended to harm him. However it had happened, she had still lost her husband and taken the life of her children's father. It had clearly had a massive impact on the whole family, and a lengthy prison sentence would only compound their collective misery. To say that there was a lot at stake would be a huge understatement.

The emotional strain of that responsibility and the fear of the consequences were etched on her face as she stood forlornly in the witness box. Her whole future would be determined over the next few days. An eerie silence hung over the court in anticipation. Her left hand was already visibly shaking as she was passed the card containing the wording of the oath. She grasped the Bible in her right hand and, in a faltering voice, said: "I swear by Almighty God that the evidence I shall give shall be the truth, the whole truth and nothing but the truth."

She took a deep breath and already looked close to tears as Jason Pitter began questioning her. Her evidence in chief took the same path as it had in June, beginning with her intentions on the night of Paul's death. She reaffirmed her assertions that the stabbing was an accident and that she had had no intention to harm him, let alone kill him. She then began sobbing, took a tissue, and wiped away the tears with her trembling right hand. After composing herself and signalling that she was okay to continue, she told the court about their relationship and their family. It had been a long and happy marriage, during which she had helped Paul through his recovery from the road accident in 1997, when the children were still young, and had nursed him back to health following his brain injury in 2010. She explained how the brain injury had changed his personality, and how not only would he drink more but it would also affect his behaviour to a greater degree. His mood would suddenly change and he would become aggressive, but she had learned to cope and it didn't bother her. She confirmed that she had made the prepared statement saying that he had been verbally and mentally abusive over the years, but said that he was never abusive in front of other people, so there was no inconsistency with what their son, Ryan, had said in his evidence. She added that she had never wanted to hurt Paul and never considered leaving him, and that their marriage was a happy one.

She was then asked about the events of 28 December 2022. She had been busy preparing the evening meal, a Mediterranean tart. The mood was good: they were playing music, and had even danced together earlier in the evening. Although they had both been drinking, Teresa claimed that she was not drunk but was concerned for her husband, as he had drunk about four glasses of wine and she thought it might spoil their evening meal. She asked him to wait until after their meal before drinking any more. He told her to shut up, called her a bitch, and said that he could drink what he liked. She told him not to talk to her like that. She admitted to shouting at him because she was angry, but said he slammed the back kitchen door and walked back into the dining room while she continued cooking the onions. She said that half of the onions were in the pan and she was chopping the other half when he stormed back into the room (note: this seemed to be a departure from her original version of the story, in which there was no mention of *cooking* onions at this stage) and shouted, "I told you, I don't want tea, chuck it in the fucking bin!"

She told the court that she had then turned to push him "out of my face". When asked what happened next, she said he had simply walked away while she finished chopping the remaining onions before placing them in the pan. She confirmed that he made no sound and that the music was still playing. She said that she first became aware that something was wrong when their dog, Kiki, began barking. She turned and looked down to see blood on the kitchen floor and Paul lying in the dining room. She said she only worked out what must have happened when she saw where the blood was coming from, but reiterated that she had only intended to push him away and wasn't conscious of having the knife in her hand at the time.

Teresa then went on to answer questions about the 999 call to summon the ambulance. She said she performed CPR on Paul and went to get a towel to stem the bleeding, and was scared and distraught while making the call and so was not thinking clearly.

When asked about her reaction to being arrested for murder, she said that she was upset, not at being arrested but because she had learned about the death of her husband and felt "dead myself". She said she didn't answer police questions because her frame of mind was "not good" and she was advised not to by her legal representative. She added that it had never crossed her mind to ignore the legal advice.

That concluded her evidence in chief, and the jury seemed a little bit stunned by what they had heard. I'm not sure if this was due to the bizarre nature of the evidence or just the tragedy of it all. Of course, the jury were the only ones who had never heard Teresa's evidence previously. They might have read about it in the papers during the first trial, but it is completely different hearing evidence live and at first hand.

It was now 1.05pm, and Judge Thackray adjourned for lunch. It is unusual to have a break halfway through giving evidence. He made it clear to Teresa that she should not discuss her evidence with anybody over lunch, including her barrister, and that she should remain in the building. The jury went for a well-earned break and I, being at the back of the court, delayed my departure until everybody else had exited. Teresa was allowed to go straight from the witness box to join her family, who then left through the court entrance and took their seats on the concourse.

The court reconvened exactly one hour after the lunch break. Alistair MacDonald had, no doubt, spent most of that time reading the notes he had taken with regard to Teresa's evidence in chief. He would have prepared meticulously, well in advance, and reviewed her evidence from the first trial. He would now be digesting what had been given in her testimony before the break and identifying any additional inconsistencies. I am sure that most of his questions were already written and rehearsed.

There is an old adage that a lawyer should never ask a question to which they do not already know the answer. A well-known mythical exchange illustrates the wisdom of this advice:

> *A man was accused of biting another man's ear off during a pub fight. His barrister was cross-examining the prosecution's key witness.*
>
> *"So, Mr Jones, the pub was quite dark, wasn't it?"*
>
> *"Yes, it was."*
>
> *"And things were very confused with all the fighting, weren't they?"*
>
> *"Yes, they were."*
>
> *"Mr Jones, I put it to you that you did not actually see the defendant bite off the man's ear. Am I correct?"*
>
> *"Well, yes."*
>
> *At this point, the barrister should have quit while he was ahead.*
>
> *"So if you didn't see him bite the ear off, why have you testified that he did it?"*
>
> *"Because I saw him spit it out."*

Once everybody had taken their places and completed the formalities, the jurors were shown to their seats and looked ready for business. Teresa entered the witness box for her cross-examination. She looked extremely apprehensive, to put it mildly. I think she knew how much rested on her evidence, and that her future, and her family's, depended on her performance against an experienced barrister. The pressure was written all over her face and manifested in her shaking arms as she brushed her hair back from her face. Her family looked on anxiously but were helpless.

Mr MacDonald rose to his feet and, without any introductory questions, went straight in.

ALISTAIR MACDONALD: Did he use the word 'bitch' to you before the head injury?

TERESA HANSON: No.

AM: Before the head injury, did you ever have to say "slow the drinking down"?

TH: No.

AM: He was never violent either before or after the injury?

TH: No.

AM: You were never afraid?

TH: No.

AM: Did he drink every night?

TH: Yes.

AM: Would he go to sleep early?

TH: Yes.

AM: [*of the head injury*] Were there any other effects?

TH: Headaches.

AM: During Covid, there were no incidents of him shouting – is that right?

TH: Yeah.

AM: Your neighbours say there were only two incidents [*arguments*]. Was it always when you told him to lay off the alcohol?

TH: Yeah.

AM: [*on the night*] Why did you tell him to ease up when you knew it would rile him?

TH: I didn't want him to spoil the tea.

AM: How much wine did he drink?

TH: Three or four glasses.

AM: How much did you have?

TH: Two or three.

AM: Where were you drinking?

TH: In the kitchen. I was getting ingredients out of the fridge while he was at the back door, smoking and singing. He then began pouring a drink from the bottle and I said, "Leave it until after tea." He said, "Don't tell me what to do!" and called me a bitch. He then said he didn't want his tea and went back into the living room. He came back a couple of minutes later and said, "I don't want tea, chuck it in the fucking bin!"

AM: How did that make you feel?

TH: I was angry with him shouting.

AM: Angry and upset?

TH: Yes.

AM: Is that why you stabbed him?

TH: I didn't know I had.

AM: You did deliberately stab him in anger, didn't you?

TH: No.

AM: Why were you trying to push him away?

TH: I didn't want him to shout at me.

Mr MacDonald then asked her to demonstrate to the jury how she had pushed Paul away. She was handed a six-inch ruler and mimed chopping onions at waist height with the ruler in her right hand before turning to her left (towards the jury) and, using both hands, pushing outwards and upwards in a gentle motion.

AM: Was the point aimed at your husband's chest?

TH: I can't remember the exact position.

AM: Did your left hand make contact with his chest?

TH: I can't remember.

AM: Did your right hand?

TH: No.

AM: You did swing that knife into his chest, didn't you?

TH: No.

AM: What was your husband's reaction?

TH: I saw him walk off out of the corner of my eye.

AM: Did you see him bent over as he walked?

TH: No.

AM: Are you saying he walked away as if nothing was wrong?

TH: Yes.

AM: You saw no reaction at all?

TH: No, I wish I had.

AM: In those ten minutes, you didn't notice the bloodstaining on the kitchen floor?

TH: No.

At this point, Teresa was sobbing under the pressure of the intensive questioning and was becoming quite distraught. She was clearly feeling very uncomfortable, and I don't think it was due only to the emotion of recounting the death of her husband.

Unbelievably, Judge Thackray decided that this was an appropriate moment to halt the cross-examination. It was only 3.05pm, and the defendant was wobbling and appeared very vulnerable. I don't know if his intervention was to spare her further distress or if there were logistical reasons to end the day prematurely. Whatever the reason, I am sure that Teresa was mightily relieved to be spared any further hostile questioning. It was rather like the referee blowing the final whistle in the midst of a goalmouth scramble in the ninety-third minute of a finely balanced cup tie. The attacking team would be furious but the defending team would be delighted that, as well as coming out with a draw, they would get a chance to regroup and would have the home advantage in the replay.

The cross-examination would have to resume the following day, giving Teresa the rest of the evening and overnight to compose herself, clear her head and prepare. This meant that she would give evidence in three separate sessions: before lunch, after lunch, and the following morning. Of course, she was not allowed to discuss the case with anybody, including her barrister, until she had completed her evidence. This was just as well, as the whole family were present in court to witness her giving evidence.

Wednesday 20 September

I doubt Teresa would have got much sleep, as she would have been reflecting on the evidence she had given. She would have spent time with her family both during the journeys to and from the court and at her parents' house, where she was bailed to stay overnight. Of course, her bail conditions and the rules of evidence would prevent her from discussing her testimony. These restrictions meant that she could only go over things in her own mind and anticipate what questions she might be asked in the remainder of her cross-examination. I wondered if she had spent time preparing her answers, as you would for a job interview. But unlike in a job interview, here it wasn't the prospect of a fresh opportunity or a pay rise on offer. The best outcome she could hope for was her liberty.

I arrived at court at 9.45am and Teresa was already in attendance with her family, sitting in a huddle on the concourse close to Court Four. Strangely, there were only two or three journalists present. I would have expected more, but there were other, more newsworthy events happening in the world, such as the ongoing war in Ukraine, the announcement of the latest inflation figures, and the King's state visit to France. Reporters frequently pool their resources for the written reports anyway and, as there was no prospect of a verdict today, there were no television cameras in attendance.

After forty-five minutes of drinking coffee, writing some notes and kicking my heels, the call came at 10.30am: "The case of Teresa Hanson."

The defendant had already taken her place in the court. Wearily, members of her family got up from their seats and made their way into the public gallery. I was a few rows further back, putting on my glasses and getting my notebook and pen ready. Alistair MacDonald and Jason Pitter were already in their places, studying papers on their desks in front of them. Judge Thackray entered the court, and the jury were shown to their seats. We were all ready for the final session of Teresa's cross-examination.

Teresa was called into the witness box once more. She looked tired, and had an expression that I thought said, Come on then, do your worst. She looked as though she was worn down by it all and just wanted it over with. Mr MacDonald opened part two of his cross-examination by asking her when she had first noticed that her husband had returned to the kitchen.

TH: I saw him come into the room from the corner of my eye as he walked round the kitchen worktop.

Mr MacDonald then read from the statement of Teresa's neighbour Shaun Trafford, who had said that he'd heard the "banging and slamming of internal doors" for ten minutes.

TH: There was only one door slammed.
AM: Are you sure?
TH: I only recall it being slammed once.
AM: You're not telling the truth, are you?
TH: I am telling the truth.
AM: What did you think when you saw the blood?
TH: I don't know what I thought.
AM: When you saw him, did you realise he was seriously injured?
TH: Yes.
AM: But you had no idea why?
TH: No. I tried to speak to him but I didn't ask him what had happened.

At this stage, Mr MacDonald became more and more incredulous and exasperated…or he appeared to. It was evident in his voice and his body language, but I don't know if it was genuine or part of the theatre of a Crown Court trial. Alistair MacDonald is an experienced barrister, and they often put on a show for the jury, with a disbelieving tone to their questions and exaggerated frustration when receiving the answers. This manifests in their facial expressions and body language: raising their eyebrows, throwing their arms in the air, shaking their head, and so on. I have been on the receiving end of this tactic from defence barristers on numerous occasions when I was merely telling the inconvenient truth. It is also designed to provoke the witness, in the hope that, even if they stick to their story, they will eventually lose their composure or even their temper. I think juries are sometimes influenced by the behaviour of the defendant. It's not just what they say but how they say it. I don't know if this was a deliberate tactic being deployed, but it was apparent that Teresa was getting rattled by the pace and nature of Mr MacDonald's questioning. This is why reading about a case in the press is no substitute for being present at a trial.

Mr MacDonald then read from the transcript of the 999 call, during which Teresa had said: "We had an argument and I stabbed him – just out of anger. We was having a row."

AM: You stabbed him in the course of an argument!
TH: [*with a raised voice*] We had an argument and I stabbed him by accident. I wasn't angry enough to kill him!
AM: You said, "I stabbed him…out of anger."

I think Mr MacDonald was perfectly aware that he was not going to get a dramatic confession. I believe he wanted to demonstrate to the jury that this 'harmless grandmother' could easily become frustrated and lose her temper. Teresa's demeanour had changed. She was no longer the vulnerable woman sobbing, dabbing her eyes with a tissue and attracting sympathy. She was clearly irritated by the nature of the questioning and had become obdurate and defiant. She was demonstrating a similar attitude to the one she had adopted during the 999 call and, perhaps, just prior to the stabbing. Her mask had slipped. It didn't need spelling out; it was there for twelve of her fellow citizens to see for themselves.

Mr MacDonald continued by asking about her prepared statement at the police station.

AM: Why was there no reference to Paul Hanson's second visit [*to the kitchen*]?
TERESA HANSON: I didn't think it was relevant.
AM: Is there any mention in the statement about pushing?
TH: No.
AM: Why not?
TH: I couldn't remember. I was distraught.

Mr MacDonald then asked her questions about the pretrial statement of defence, in which she had changed her account and claimed that the stabbing had occurred while she was attempting to push her husband away. As expected, there were no revealing answers, just replies to the effect that she wasn't thinking straight and was distraught when she gave her prepared statement at the police station. She insisted that the defence statement was a true account of what had happened. At this moment, I think Mr MacDonald realised that there was nothing more to be gained, and wanted Teresa's loss of composure to be the lasting memory for the jury. He sat down and left Mr Pitter to pick up the pieces in a re-examination.

There was an extended pause with what I would call an embarrassed silence. It's like when you are the guests of another couple, who have an argument in your presence: you daren't say anything, but you can't simply walk out and leave them. I'm not sure that a re-examination was really necessary, but I think Mr Pitter felt as if he couldn't leave things as they were. He asked a few simple questions in a noticeably calm and sympathetic manner, the purpose being to allow Teresa to regain her composure and to 'tidy up' and clarify a few of her less convincing responses.

It was now 11.30am, and there was a break for what was described by the judge as a "legal issue". After the jury left the courtroom, there was a minor spat between the two barristers. Mr Pitter complained that his opposite number had claimed that the defendant had deliberately delayed calling the emergency services and therefore delayed Paul's treatment. Mr MacDonald denied this, saying that it was the defendant herself who'd admitted to a delay of ten minutes before dialling 999 as she was cooking the onions. He hadn't said or implied that this was deliberate. My own thoughts were that Mr MacDonald hadn't intended to give this impression, and that the defendant couldn't have it both ways. You can't on the one hand claim that for ten minutes you didn't notice that you'd stabbed your husband, and then on the other hand complain about the prosecution highlighting the delay. If anything, I think the prosecuting barrister was implying the opposite: that she *hadn't* delayed calling for help, but had invented the story of cooking the onions for her own convenience. The judge advised them to sort it out and come to a compromise – hence the break.

After a twenty-minute interval, we returned to Court Four to hear the remainder of the defence case. Messrs Pitter and MacDonald had sorted out their differences and issued a statement of clarification to the jury.

Sherri Hanson

The next witness for the defence was Teresa and Paul's daughter, Sherri. As you would expect, her testimony was more or less identical to the one she had given in the first trial, except that this time it sounded a bit more desperate. Having just sat through her mother's evidence, I think she realised that things weren't going well.

As Jason Pitter gently led her through her evidence, she told the jury, with a pained expression, that her mother had thought the world of her father: they did everything together and were inseparable. Sherri had never seen her mother acting aggressively towards her father, verbally or physically. She was utterly devoted to him as well as being a loving mother and grandmother. Once again, when asked about the possibility of her mother deliberately harming her father, Sherri repeated the phrase she'd used in the original trial: "Impossible – she loved him too much." Although her lines appeared to be well rehearsed, they were delivered with noticeably less confidence. It was more of a plea from the heart than it was evidence. As if to confirm this observation, she completed her testimony by emotionally declaring, "It's awful to see how much pain she is in without him." You couldn't help feeling sympathy. On Christmas Day she had posted on Facebook, "We've had the best day today with family." Three days later her mother had killed her father, and now she faced losing her mother too.

There was nothing left to be said. Alistair MacDonald seemed to share this view, as he declined the opportunity of a cross-examination. What could he have asked her? Sherri left the witness box with tears in her eyes and appeared to be overcome with emotion as she returned to the public gallery and rejoined what remained of her family.

Vanessa Lappin

Vanessa is Paul's elder sister, who gave evidence of Teresa's good character in the first trial. Other than his children, she was the only blood relative of Paul to give evidence in the original trial. On this occasion, she was absent. We were told that the absence was due to illness, and we had to accept that. In lieu of her live testimony, her written statement was read to the court.

In order to have a witness's statement read out in court, it must be 'agreed' by the prosecution, in which case there must be no need for cross-examination of the evidence. As there had been no cross-examination during the first trial, why had Vanessa given her evidence in person? If she was required to give live testimony in the first trial, why was it permitted to have her evidence read out now? It just adds weight to my theory that the defence wanted her to be present because of *who* she was.

The jury was told that Vanessa was very close to her brother and had known Teresa for thirty-seven years, since she and Paul began courting. Paul was very happy being married to Teresa, who was a kind and caring wife. Teresa and Paul had both helped Vanessa through a difficult time in the past, for which she was extremely grateful. Finally, Vanessa's statement emphasised what a loving mother and doting grandmother Teresa was.

Four further statements were then read to the jury, all giving evidence of Teresa's character. These were mainly from close family friends. They were all fairly similar, with each saying once again what a loving, caring wife and mother she was. This concluded the case for the defence.

27

The Judge's Directions

At 12.50pm, there was just enough time before lunch for the judge to give his directions to the jury. It is for the jury to decide what is fact, and it is the judge's role to guide them in matters of law. When there is conflicting evidence – as in this case – the jury have to decide who to believe (or which version of events is more likely to be true) and give their verdict accordingly. The default position here was that the defendant was not guilty unless the jury were sure, beyond reasonable doubt, that she was guilty of one of the two offences: murder or manslaughter. The judge's directions immediately precede the closing speeches of the prosecution and the defence, and provide a template for the jury's deliberations.

Judge Thackray asked the jury to consider:

- the conduct of the defendant
- whether her actions were deliberate or accidental
- if deliberate, what was her intention?

He instructed the jury to:

- put emotion to one side
- not speculate about anything
- ignore the fact that this was a retrial.

He then spoke about the specific offences, and immediately ruled out any thoughts of self-defence.

Murder

Judge Thackray informed the jury that in order to convict for murder, they must be satisfied that there was an intention to kill or do serious harm and that the wound had been inflicted deliberately.

Manslaughter

To be guilty of manslaughter, the defendant must have intended or foreseen that she would cause *some* physical harm, but not *serious* physical harm.

He then told the jury not to attach any significance to Teresa's failure to answer police questions. "She was upset and not familiar with police procedure."

Finally, Judge Thackray invited the jury to take into consideration the substantial amount of character evidence they had heard.

It was now 1.05pm. The court adjourned for lunch, and the judge instructed everybody to return at 2.20pm.

28

The Closing Speech of the Prosecution

Everybody had taken their seats promptly, and the jury were shown to their places at exactly 2.20pm. Time was clearly still an issue, because with the minimum of formality and delay the prosecuting counsel, Alistair MacDonald, was invited to make his closing speech.

He rose to his feet, adjusted his glasses and, after a quick glance at his notes, asked the jury in a disbelieving tone: "Whatever her desire, what else could her intention have been? Paul Hanson was a loving father, grandfather and husband. It was drink that made him verbally abusive. The defendant herself says that it [verbal abuse] only ever happened when he'd been drinking. She had never thought of leaving him, and there was no suggestion of violence or that she was even afraid of him. What set him off was when she told him not to drink until after tea. Mrs Hanson's technique when the going gets tough is to say, 'Oh, I can't remember, it was all a blur.'"

Mr MacDonald then reminded the jury of the research presented in the evidence of Dr Parsons. "In the two studies, an accidental stabbing with a knife has never happened. It is theoretically possible, but nobody can say there won't ever be a case of a plane crashing in Leeds city centre. There are millions of flights in and out of Leeds Bradford Airport every year, but it has never happened."

He then spoke about the incident itself, with an exaggerated sense of incredulity as his voice moved up an octave and his statements became questions. "He never moaned or said anything?

He was bent over double, heavily bleeding, and the trail of blood started only about a metre from where she was standing? She carried on chopping onions with the same knife covered in body fat and tissue? She spent ten minutes cooking onions and unrolled the pastry while only a few feet away was the trail of blood, and for ten minutes she didn't look up and say, 'What's that?' She didn't know anything about her husband falling and lying on the floor until Kiki the dog started barking? She claims that even when she found him, she didn't know if he'd had a heart attack and only knew [it was a stabbing] when she checked under his clothing to find the wound in his chest?"

Mr MacDonald then moved on by quoting from the 999 call, the contents of which, of course, cannot be disputed:

TERESA HANSON: We had an argument and I stabbed him.
CALL TAKER: Who was it that stabbed him?
TH: It was just out of anger – I was just making fucking tea.

Mr MacDonald then drew the jury's attention to the official defence statement, which was made on 31 May 2023. This was five months after the incident, but only twelve days before the first trial. He pointed out that this version of events was significantly different from Teresa's prepared statement given at the police station after her arrest. In her original statement she had claimed that Paul had simply walked onto the knife, but in her defence statement this had changed to her accidentally stabbing him while trying to push him away, not realising that she had the knife in her hand.

Crucially, Mr MacDonald then reminded the jury of the contents of the next-door neighbour's statement. Shaun Trafford said that he had heard the slamming of doors for about ten minutes and that there had then been a significant gap before he saw the ambulance arrive at the scene at 7.22pm. (This is the time the ambulance crew actually entered the property. Shaun Trafford, who appears to be mistaken with his timings, claimed the slamming of doors began at about 7.20pm. It had lasted approximately ten minutes and was then followed by a significant time gap before the ambulance arrived.) Teresa claimed that the door was slammed only once.

Mr MacDonald then completed his summing up by addressing the jury directly: 'Does she really expect you to believe that she failed completely to notice that her husband, who must have been just a few paces away, was bent double, moving away from her? She didn't notice any of that? She just went on calmly cutting onions with the same knife? Is it credible that in his death agony, he moved out of that kitchen and said absolutely nothing? He didn't sigh, groan or gasp, didn't say, 'Teresa, what have you done to me?' He just walked out of the kitchen, she said – she didn't realise anything was wrong.'

It was now 3.20pm, so the prosecution's closing speech had taken a whole hour. What I have written above is merely a summary of the main points put forward by Mr MacDonald. During his speech, I occasionally observed the jury to try to read their body language. It was noticeable that there was a great deal of active listening going on. It was also very apparent that about half of the jury were doing a lot of writing, so I imagine their notes were, similarly to mine, a summary of the main points.

29

The Closing Speech of the Defence

It was now the turn of Jason Pitter to make the case for the defence in the form of his closing speech to the jury. The defence barrister stands closest to the jury, and he seemed to exploit that advantage by turning to face the twelve men and women to make eye contact whenever he could.

As expected, his main theme was the lack of motive. He talked about Paul and Teresa being the centre of each other's worlds. "Why would she want to cause him serious harm?" was the rhetorical question. He appeared to be attempting to appeal to the jury's emotions rather than their cognitive judgement of the evidence before saying, "We don't say that from an emotional perspective, but based on the evidence. That person who nursed him through serious ill health [the road accident] suddenly wants to do him serious harm? That simply doesn't add up. She was a devoted and loving wife and mother who took pride in putting others' needs before her own."

I glanced across at the jury. They didn't seem to be taking many notes this time. Some were twiddling with their pens. As far as I could see, nobody was engaging with Mr Pitter, and most were trying to avoid eye contact.

He continued regardless. "The prosecution suggest that she cold-heartedly ignored what had happened [they didn't] and calmly carried on preparing tea, leaving her husband on the floor, bleeding."

Mr Pitter concluded his closing speech by quoting from the recording of the 999 call. This was a surprise, as I would have thought that that would be something he would be keen to avoid. "'He called me a bitch so I…I don't know what I did.'" I can only think that this was to suggest that because the call was made in the immediate aftermath of the stabbing, she had been consistent from the beginning in claiming that it was an accident. My interpretation was that it did the opposite by emphasising the link between being called a bitch and stabbing Paul. It also highlighted the fact that there was no mention of her pushing him away or him walking onto the knife.

After making his final earnest appeal to the jury, Mr Pitter sat down at 4.05pm. His speech had lasted forty-five minutes. We had gone all afternoon without a break, and the time seemed right to adjourn until tomorrow. Judge Thackray, though, had other ideas, and announced that he would now begin his summing up. I can only guess that he wanted to make up for lost time and wanted the case finished and dealt with by the end of the week.

30

The Judge's Summing Up

I think the jury had had enough by now, but Judge Thackray ploughed on regardless. He began by talking about the background of the couple. Teresa and Paul had met on the college bus in 1985 and had married in 1989. In 1997 Paul had suffered a serious injury following a major car accident, from which Teresa had nursed him back to health. They were soulmates, with no history of violence between them. Following Paul's assault in 2010, in which he sustained a brain injury, he drank more and got drunk more easily. Despite this, the defendant again cared for him, and was supportive and tolerant.

Judge Thackray then moved on to the build-up to the incident. The whole family had enjoyed a wonderful Christmas Day. On 27 December, Paul had watched movies with his two young grandsons. The following day, he and Teresa had booked a holiday and visited her sister-in-law before going to the local supermarket to buy something for their evening meal. Immediately before the incident, their neighbour heard the slamming of doors for ten minutes before it all went quiet.

Judge Thackray then posed the question to the jury: "Was it a tragic accident or a tragic homicide? If it was homicide, was it murder or manslaughter?" He reminded the jury of the 999 call made by the defendant:

TERESA HANSON: We had an argument and I stabbed him
– just out of anger. We was having a row… He told me to fuck
off and called me a bitch so I…I don't know what I did.

Judge Thackray then gave a precis of the evidence of the
forensic pathologist, who had concluded that for a stabbing to occur
in the manner described by Teresa would be "highly unlikely".

The judge then talked about the investigation, referring to
the prepared statement and Teresa's decision not to answer police
questions other than to reply "no comment". He repeated his advice
not to attach any significance to this, as she was acting on legal
advice and was unfamiliar with police procedure.

He completed his summing up by highlighting the evidence
from numerous character witnesses, who had all said that Teresa was
a loving and caring wife, mother and grandmother.

It was now approaching 4.30pm, and Judge Thackray decided
that this was an appropriate moment to adjourn proceedings until
the next day. It had been a very long session, beginning with the cross-
examination of Teresa, followed by the rest of the defence evidence,
and finishing off with the judge's directions, the prosecution and
defence closing speeches, and the judge's own summing up. There
had been a lot for the jury to digest in one day. Their heads must
have been spinning, and if they had taken as many notes as I had,
they had probably run out of paper.

The reason for the late sitting then became clear. Judge
Thackray announced that proceedings would recommence at 1pm
the next day. There was to be no morning session, so another half-
day was lost. I am assuming that he or one of the barristers had a
prearranged appointment that couldn't be cancelled, although this
wasn't mentioned in open court. It was unusual to finish so late,
and Judge Thackray seemed desperate to ensure that this case didn't
enter a third week. The jury were shown out of Court Four, and the

rest of us felt very weary as we made our way out of the almost empty court building to join Hull's busy rush-hour traffic.

Thursday 21 September

With the late start, I could at least have a relaxing morning at home, reading through my copious notes from the previous day. I enjoyed an early lunch before setting off at midday, arriving at court at 12.45pm. The security screening area was quieter at this time and I had no packed lunch to declare, so the process was much quicker than normal.

As I sat on the concourse, I was resigned to the fact that our planned early morning trip the next day to see Suzi Quatro would have to be delayed. I didn't think I would get away with cancelling it altogether, as it was our anniversary, so I was hoping that the case would be completed by no later than lunchtime on Friday. If it went beyond this, I would almost certainly miss the most important and dramatic part of the trial: the verdict. But as I glanced across at Teresa and her family, I realised how lucky I was that this was the only issue causing me anxiety. For them, the next two days would change all of their lives one way or the other. How were they coping with the stress and worry? I know from personal experience how upsetting it is to lose a parent. Ryan and Sherri had had this hanging over them for nine months, and probably hadn't grieved properly for their father yet. They now faced the possibility of losing their mother too.

"The case of Teresa Hanson."

It was 1pm on the dot as we all filed into court. I hung back to give the family as much time and space as I possibly could. I sensed an atmosphere. There was very little chat between them as the gravity of the situation became real. I quietly sat down on the very back row of the public gallery, took out my notebook and pen, and put on my glasses. Teresa assumed her position in the screened-off area at the back of the court, accompanied by a security guard.

The barristers were in their places and the jury were shown to their seats before Judge Thackray entered the court.

"All rise."

We got to our feet and waited for Judge Thackray to be seated before taking our places once again.

The judge immediately got into his stride by giving the jury the route to verdict. This was a virtual repeat of the instructions issued to the first jury in June, which can be summarised as follows:

1. Was it a deliberate stabbing? If not, you must find the defendant not guilty of both murder and manslaughter.

2. If you consider it to have been a deliberate stabbing, are you sure that the defendant intended to cause serious harm? If not, she is not guilty of murder.

3. If not serious harm, did she intend to cause *some* harm? If the answer to that question is yes, then you must find her guilty of manslaughter. If the answer is no, she is not guilty of manslaughter.

Judge Thackray then told the jury that he required a unanimous verdict. He said that they should all reconvene in court at 4.10pm.

As I looked across at the jury they seemed very attentive, with several writing notes and looking very serious. It is a huge responsibility. Judge Thackray's legal directions were very clear. It was now completely down to them to decide on the matter of guilt or innocence. There was a lot to consider, and it seemed to have been a long time since they were sworn in. Twelve strangers of different ages and backgrounds, unexpectedly thrown together to discuss the merits of the evidence. Were they all of a similar mind, or would they be split, as in the original trial? I think the defence would have settled for a hung jury, as it was doubtful that there would be a fourth trial. It was 1.25pm, and the jury retired to consider their verdict. Interestingly, they were allowed to take a court laptop into the jury room so that they could listen to the recordings of the 999 calls. I don't remember this happening in the first trial. The six men and six women were escorted by a jury usher as they slowly and silently walked out of the court, a huge weight on their shoulders.

We all stood up as the judge exited the court and returned to his private chambers. There were surprisingly few reporters in attendance, as nobody was anticipating a verdict until tomorrow at the earliest. The family left the courtroom and were soon joined by Teresa. She went down the stairs, accompanied by her son and daughter. This may have been to get a coffee, or she may have gone outside for some fresh air. It might be her last chance for some years to experience freedom and to spend time alone with her children. How must she be feeling? What could her family say or do to raise her morale during the long wait for a verdict?

After exiting the court, I took my seat on the concourse. Ten minutes later, after Teresa had returned, I looked up and did a double take. Was that Jason Pitter in a civilian coat, heading for the stairs? Where was he going? Knowing that a long wait was inevitable, perhaps he was just popping out for something to eat? He stopped and talked to the family, and I'm sure he was apologising and saying something like his junior would look after them. My initial thoughts were that if he was leaving early, there was absolutely no chance of a verdict today.

I was joined by two reporters. One was a local newspaper journalist and the other a regional television reporter. They were debating whether or not it was worth sticking around until 'close of play'. I said that since I'd got this far I might as well hang about until the end. The newspaper man, who, I believe, lived locally, said that he would be staying anyway. I then told the television reporter that I'd seen Mr Pitter leave ten minutes earlier. That was it – the television reporter was adamant that he was leaving, as he had a long way to travel home. It was then that Alistair MacDonald walked past, still in his wig and gown. The television reporter couldn't resist, and went straight up to him to ask what was going on. I wouldn't have had the nerve, but I suppose that's his job. Apparently, Mr MacDonald confirmed Mr Pitter's departure and said he thought it was unlikely there would be a verdict today. The television reporter was virtually putting his coat on after hearing this. He said he'd have to type up his report, and if he left now he could beat the traffic and do it from home. The three of us got talking and were speculating about the likely verdict when the television reporter said, "I might as well stay now," and we all got a coffee. He was typing up his report as we carried on gossiping among ourselves.

After another half-hour, we saw Mr MacDonald traversing the concourse as though he meant business. What was happening? He returned to the barristers' office with a sense of urgency, and was once again accosted by the television reporter, who asked him what was going on. Apparently, the judge had given the jury an extension to 4.30pm. Something was *definitely* going on.

31

The Verdict

By about 4.10pm, there was a flurry of activity outside Court Four. The clerk and the ushers were scurrying about, and Alistair MacDonald entered the court, followed by Helen Chapman, who was Jason Pitter's junior and had assisted him throughout the trial.

It was all too much for the television reporter, who couldn't contain himself any longer. "I'm going to find out what's happening." He walked straight over to the entrance to Court Four and disappeared down the corridor.

I looked across at the family, who were still seated outside, apparently none the wiser. I thought it best to wait for the official call, and in any case, nothing was going to happen while the family were still sitting on the concourse. Still, I couldn't relax, because it was obvious that something was about to happen. I kept looking over towards the court entrance, with half an eye on the family, who remained seated. I then saw the television reporter emerge from the entrance, waving frantically to gain my attention. Once we had made eye contact, he vigorously beckoned me over. I threw all my things into my bag and walked straight over, followed by the newspaper journalist. We walked towards the family, who still appeared to be oblivious to the frantic activity going on around them. As we passed them, I could see in my peripheral vision that they were watching us. They must have realised at this point that the court was about to sit again. It appeared that nobody had bothered to tell them.

We were greeted by the television reporter, who said, quite excitedly, "They've reached a verdict!" It was very kind of him to take the trouble to come out and let us know. I bet he was glad he didn't leave early. The jury had reached a verdict in just two hours and forty-five minutes.

I went straight to my seat at the back of the public gallery. Reporters began taking their seats on the press bench. I was expecting the court to be full, but there were only the 'usual suspects' who had attended regularly. I don't think any of the occasional attendees had expected a verdict today; neither had we – but our patience had been rewarded. I never did hear an official announcement about the case, but with everybody piling into Court Four as though it were the January sales (but with less decorum), I doubt an announcement was necessary. It appeared that the family were the last to find out, but maybe they deliberately waited to wish Teresa luck – and, perhaps, say goodbye.

They eventually made a dignified group entrance and took their customary seats towards the front while Teresa took her place at the back of the court, closely accompanied by a security guard as she waited to hear her fate. The barristers had taken their positions: Alistair MacDonald was nearest to us, and in Jason Pitter's absence Helen Chapman had been promoted to the front bench nearest the jury. The clerk was on the telephone, informing the judge that everything was ready. The usher was nervously fussing around, making sure that everything was as it should be.

"All rise," said the clerk as Judge Thackray entered the courtroom from his private quarters.

Everybody rose as one and retook their seats once the judge had made himself comfortable. The family were, understandably, nervous and fidgety. This was the moment. After nine months of waiting and three trials, they were about to hear the outcome. I can only describe the atmosphere as electric. The tension was almost palpable. I had never experienced a feeling like it and I had nothing vested in the outcome, so it is impossible to imagine what Teresa's family were feeling.

The jury usher escorted the six men and six women to their seats on the opposite side of the court, and they calmly sat down. The clerk walked across and asked the foreperson to make themself known. A younger, bespectacled man rose to his feet.

"Have you reached a verdict upon which you all agree?" asked the clerk.

"Yes," replied the foreperson.

The packed court went absolutely silent. As well as being able to hear a pin drop, you could probably have heard a feather drop.

"On the charge of murder, do you find the defendant guilty or not guilty?"

"Guilty."

There was a momentary pause of disbelief, followed by shrieks and cries of "*No!*" from the family in front of me. It was difficult to know which way to look, but I caught a glimpse of Teresa, who had a look of shock on her face before putting her head in her hands. An older man in front of me, whom I assumed to be her father, declared loudly, "Unbelievable!" The jury appeared to agree, but what they considered to be unbelievable was Teresa's evidence. The person I assumed to be her father was, of course, referring to the verdict. The shrieks from the front of the public gallery gradually turned to sobbing and embracing as the realisation of what had just happened began to sink in. Teresa Hanson, the loving, caring, doting mother and grandmother, was now a convicted murderer.

After allowing time for people to regain their composure, Judge Thackray addressed Teresa directly. "You have been convicted of murder. You know that there is only one sentence, which is life imprisonment."

There were more gasps from the family in front of me.

The judge then addressed the barristers with regard to the date for the sentencing hearing. After perusing their respective diaries, a date was agreed. It was to be Tuesday 3 October. Of course, there would be no bail granted, as Teresa was now a convicted prisoner starting her custodial sentence. She would shortly be escorted downstairs through the cell area to a waiting prison van for her onward journey to jail. Thursday 21 September was day one of her prison sentence.

Being at the back of the public gallery, I decided to wait until everybody else had left the court before making my move. The family were still clearly in shock. Nobody wanted to go first, but eventually the police officers in attendance got to their feet and headed for the exit. Their path took them in front of the public gallery, and as they filed past, the older man I believed to be Teresa's father shouted across to them in a sardonic tone, "Yeah, that's it, off you go." I don't know exactly what he meant by this, but he obviously thought that the police had let the family down. Did he think that, following a fatal stabbing, the police should investigate and do their best to secure an acquittal? His ire was almost certainly aimed at the poor FLO, who was in the unenviable position of supporting the victim's family, who also happened to be the family of the defendant. If Paul had been killed by a stranger, the family would have been thanking the police for securing a murder conviction – but blood is thicker than water.

After the police officers left the court, the family began to depart. Obviously, at this stage emotions were running high. I thought it would be discreet to hold well back before making my exit. The man I assumed to be Teresa's father seemed to be looking for somebody on whom he could take out his anger and frustration. I didn't want to be that person. After a few minutes I made my way out, and I was relieved that all the members of the Hanson family appeared to have left.

Following the verdict, the senior investigating officer, DCI Nicola Burnett (who was not present to hear the verdict announced), was quoted as saying, "The family has been through a harrowing ordeal but violence will not be accepted in any guise. We will always do everything we can to seek justice for those who come to harm at the hands of another, and to ensure those who commit the crime are held to account for their actions. In this case, a verbal argument spiralled out of control and as a result of Teresa's actions that day, her husband lost his life. This has been an incredibly difficult investigation that has left a family utterly devastated. I would please ask that their privacy be respected during this traumatic time."

Most of the reporters had shot off to break the dramatic news of the verdict. I said my farewells to the one or two who were remaining, but didn't hang around as I knew they had work to do, and I wanted to get home and listen to the news.

On my way home it dawned on me that, because of the earlier-than-expected verdict, my Friday was free. My wife and I were able to set off early for our weekend away without me missing any of the trial. We had a marvellous weekend and enjoyed watching Suzi Quatro perform just like I remember her doing in my schooldays, fifty years previously. I hope I still have the same energy when *I'm* seventy-three.

32

The Sentencing Hearing

I attended the court again on Tuesday 3 October, when Teresa was due to be sentenced at 10am. There was a long delay, the reason for which was not explained. During this time I pondered over the likely sentence and wondered what a lengthy prison sentence is supposed to achieve. Generally, as I see it, imprisonment has four potential purposes, and very rarely do all of them apply:

1. To punish.
2. To protect the public.
3. To act as a deterrent.
4. To rehabilitate.

On the one hand, Teresa's children had lost their father and were now about to in effect lose their mother too. The family were supporting Teresa throughout the trial, and nobody (as far as I am aware) was demanding a long sentence on behalf of her late husband. Who speaks on Paul's behalf? Were there other family members who were less supportive but chose not to give evidence or attend court? I don't know. What would Paul himself have thought of it? We will never know. Nobody can bring him back, and the situation has to be dealt with as it is.

Is Teresa Hanson, a (now) fifty-four-year-old wife, mother and grandmother of previous good character, a danger to the public? Hardly. Does she need rehabilitating? I don't think so. So if protection of the public and rehabilitation do not apply in this case, that only leaves the deterrent and punishment aspects. Would a long sentence act as a deterrent to others thinking of doing away with their partner? Possibly. Does Teresa deserve to be punished? Certainly, because she has to be held accountable for her actions and the public demand it.

The wider family have already had their lives devastated, and they haven't done anything wrong. On the other hand, being found guilty of murder requires a long prison sentence. The public expect it. Murder is perhaps the most serious crime that can be committed, even if, as in this case, it was a one-off event in unusual circumstances. I don't believe for a minute that even in the heat of the moment Teresa intended to kill Paul, but if she deliberately plunged a knife into his chest, her only intention must have been to cause him serious harm. That's what the jury decided.

If this offence had occurred before 1965, she could have faced the death penalty. In the United Kingdom, capital punishment was abolished on the understanding that a life sentence would be mandatory for the offence of murder. It still is a life *sentence*, but a minimum tariff of *imprisonment* is now determined by the judge. Once the minimum term has been served, the prisoner is eligible to spend the remainder of their sentence on licence in the community. This decision is made by the parole board and is based on whether they consider them safe for release. Any breach of the licence would mean a recall to prison, where they could, potentially, serve the remainder of their life sentence. Only in very rare and extreme cases does the defendant receive a 'whole life' tariff. One recent example is the case of Lucy Letby, the nurse found guilty of murdering babies in her care. I believe that Teresa genuinely regrets her actions when she 'snapped' on that fateful night. In October 2023, the latest figures from the Ministry of Justice informed us that the cost to the public of imprisoning somebody is slightly under £50,000 a year. Is this money well spent in a case like this? I also read that there were more than 88,000 inmates in British prisons – a record high – and judges had been requested to delay sentencing, and politicians were exploring ways of releasing inmates early.

We were called into court at 11.05am. The procedure is that both prosecution and defence counsels make their representations to the judge in relation to any aggravating or mitigating factors, hoping to influence the minimum term the prisoner should serve. In less complex cases like Teresa's, where the crime wasn't planned in advance, was not a repeat offence, and didn't involve a firearm, the starting point is a minimum of fifteen years' imprisonment. Any reduction of or extension to this term has to be justified by citing aggravating or mitigating circumstances as per the Sentencing Act 2020.

We were again in Court Four. For the first time in this case, the court was packed. All of the family were in attendance, as they had been faithfully on every day of the three trials, and they took their seats towards the front of the public gallery. The small area reserved for the press was fully occupied, with other journalists having to sit among the relatives and the police. The three police officers who had attended regularly during the trials were now joined by a woman who, I assumed, was DCI Nicola Burnett, the senior investigating officer, who hadn't been present for the verdict. I took my usual seat at the back of the public gallery behind the relatives, from where I could just see the dock through a small gap in the screen. Several other people, whom I didn't recognise, were also in the public gallery. I assumed they were either representatives of the press or technical staff from the television news. Teresa, who was now in custody and would have been transferred from prison to attend the sentencing hearing, entered the dock from the holding area at 11.08am. She wore a black and white patterned dress, a black cardigan and, as ever, her wedding ring. She had her hair tied up and, for the first time, she was wearing glasses. Her relatives immediately turned to face her, smiled, waved and blew kisses. This was reciprocated by Teresa. Alistair MacDonald and Jason Pitter were poised and waiting to make their representations. The atmosphere was tense and nobody dared speak, rather like in a dentist's waiting room. The clerk of the court seemed to be having trouble getting through to the judge on the internal telephone system. Looking rather flustered, he then went 'backstage', presumably to inform Judge Thackray that everybody was in court and waiting.

After what seemed like an age, Judge Thackray entered the court to the now familiar routine of the clerk's instruction of "all rise" and everybody responding by getting to their feet and retaking their seats only after the judge had sat down.

Proceedings began with Teresa's son, Ryan, standing in the witness box, having been granted permission to give a victim personal statement (VPS). He made this statement on behalf of himself and his sister, Sherri. The VPS was created to give people affected by crime the opportunity to tell the court the impact it has had on their lives, and it may be taken into consideration by the judge when deciding the sentence. It outlines the devastating effects of the crime, and can be a way of addressing the defendant directly. It is normally also an attempt to encourage the judge to hand out the harshest possible sentence, but on this occasion the defendant was, of course, Ryan and Sherri's own mother, and so their VPS was an attempt to persuade Judge Thackray to give as short a sentence as he could, directly appealing for leniency on Teresa's behalf.

Ryan was softly spoken and difficult to hear from the back of the court. He either refused to believe that his father's death was a crime or just couldn't bring himself to use that term or more specific words such as 'stabbing' or 'killing', and certainly not 'murder'. He began, "Since the accident, our worlds have changed forever." He went on to tell the court how close they all were as a family, and how he and Sherri were now grieving the loss not only of their father but also of their mother. He talked about the integral part both of his parents had played in the care and upbringing of their grandchildren. He described the financial impact of having to pay for childcare and taking so much time off work. He spoke movingly about his sister, Sherri, who had discovered that she was pregnant just prior to the incident in December, and who had recently given birth to their parents' first granddaughter – a granddaughter whom their father would never know about and whom their mother would rarely see. He then pleaded with the judge to be lenient and take into account his and Sherri's views when sentencing.

In response, Judge Thackray said, "I can assure you I will take into account your feelings, but I also have to take into account the public interest and the wider picture."

It was now time for Mr MacDonald to make his representations, and following Ryan's speech a heavy, sombre mood hung over the court. It felt more like a funeral than a sentencing hearing. It actually felt a bit awkward. It was as though the judge and the two barristers were thinking, This is a bit of a mess – how are we going to resolve this? As per the official CPS guidance, during sentencing the adversarial procedure is suspended and the prosecutor adopts a neutral stance by acting in the public interest. It was really a case of working together to reach an agreement that was fair and would satisfy all parties. Mr MacDonald began by stating Teresa's age and the fact that she was of previous good character. He reiterated the minimum starting point being fifteen years' imprisonment, but reminded the judge of her time in police custody, the three days she had spent on remand, and the curfew to which she was subjected while on bail, which, astonishingly, can all be added up and counted as part of her term in prison under Section 240 of the Criminal Justice Act 2003. He then mentioned the further pain suffered by the victim caused by Teresa's delay in calling for help, pointing out that this didn't have to be deliberate to be considered an aggravating factor.

Judge Thackray then spoke of numerous mitigating factors, such as the lack of premeditation and the fact that he was satisfied that there was no intention to kill. He talked of the Hansons' long and happy marriage and the occasions when Teresa had provided care and assistance to Paul following his two serious injuries. He also promised to take into account the family's wishes in terms of clemency and leniency.

It was now Mr Pitter's turn to make representations on behalf of the defence. He began by saying that he had no words to describe the tragedy but suggested that, in addition to the factors already mentioned, there were other issues he believed should be regarded as mitigating factors. Teresa had now been diagnosed as suffering from post-traumatic stress disorder (PTSD) and was having frequent nightmares. She was remorseful for her actions and didn't seek to blame Paul for them. Mr Pitter also pointed out the irony of Teresa nursing her husband back to health following the brain injury, which was a significant factor in his behaviour which had led to the stabbing. Mr Pitter completed his speech by requesting a significant reduction on the starting point for the minimum term.

The judge then finished the morning session by stating what everybody already knew, namely that it was an "extraordinarily difficult sentencing exercise". He then adjourned the court at 11.40am and said he would sentence Teresa at 2pm. She was taken down to the cells, waving to her family as she went. This seems a long break, but I imagine that time is needed for the judge to check a few legal aspects of the sentencing, make his decision and to write the report.

After the extended lunch break, we were called back into court at exactly 2pm. I had made a few notes before enjoying lunch and had breathed some fresh air. The journalists and reporters were already writing their scripts for their websites, newspapers and television reports; I imagine they had just left space for the judge's remarks and a gap before the words 'years' imprisonment'. The court was full, as you would expect, but this time extra space had been created on the press bench to accommodate the increased interest by removing some old furniture and equipment that had previously been stored there. The regular attendees took their usual seats as Teresa was led into the dock. What must she be thinking? After all that had happened, her fate would be known in the next ten minutes.

Judge Thackray entered the courtroom and, after the standing-up-and-sitting-down ritual, confirmed the prisoner's name, gave her permission to remain seated, and began his speech. "The court is sitting today to sentence Teresa Hanson following your conviction for murder."

He then explained that the punishment was fixed by law and that it was a life sentence. "A minimum term of imprisonment must be served before being referred to the parole board to be released on licence. For my part, I conclude you pose no risk to the public whatsoever or are likely to in the future. If released, you can be recalled.

"You were, to coin a phrase, childhood sweethearts, and from then on until his death were utterly devoted to each other. You married in 1989 and had two children. It was evident you were an exceptionally close family and your children were as devoted to you and your husband as you were devoted to them and their children.

"The tragic circumstances of your case demonstrate in the clearest terms the danger of wielding a knife and using it. The use of knives causes particular concern, partly because carrying knives is all too common, and partly because, in a domestic context, kitchen knives are readily accessible and provide a convenient and deadly weapon. Part of this sentencing exercise is to discourage the use of such a weapon even in the context of a relatively spontaneous act.

"You were both amazing parents and grandparents and they [the children] honestly believed that the idea of you wanting to harm your husband was inconceivable."

Judge Thackray then talked about the evening of 27 December (he meant the 28th), and said that Paul was a large man – six feet tall (he was actually five feet six inches) and weighing fifteen stone (actually fourteen stone and eleven pounds). "Having presided over your trial, I am satisfied there was a large element of provocation… It was a spontaneous act of violence, but you did intend serious harm, which you immediately regretted… Part of the sentencing exercise is to discourage the use of knives, even in a domestic context… I must act in the public interest with the widespread use of knives. Paul Hanson lost his life due to your criminal act. His provocation did not justify your actions."

Judge Thackray then went on to explain that the starting point for sentencing was fifteen years, plus or minus aggravating or mitigating factors. With regard to the only suggested aggravating factor – the prolonged agony suffered by Paul due to the delay in receiving treatment – the judge dismissed it immediately by saying that he was satisfied that the suffering lasted "no more than a few seconds". He then listed the mitigating factors he would be taking into consideration:

- good character
- no intention to kill
- lack of premeditation
- provocation.

He praised Teresa for seeking to protect her husband's reputation by playing down his aggressive behaviour, and acknowledged that she had recently been diagnosed with PTSD and was having frequent nightmares.

"You will serve a minimum term of imprisonment of nine years."

There was a muted response from the court, and particularly from the family. Of course, they would have known that she would be going to prison for a long time, and they had already had time to process that reality. I suspect there was an element of relief: it could have been worse, and nine years was probably a shorter term than they were expecting. (Soon after the sentencing hearing, the prosecution indicated that they would launch an appeal against what they considered to be an 'unduly lenient' sentence.)[1] The family turned to wave to Teresa before she was led down, and then they quietly left the courtroom. I remained in my seat to give them time and space. The media people also remained seated and were handed a paper copy of the judge's verdict, which is a kind of press release. It was calculated that Teresa should be credited for her time in police custody, on remand, and for the curfew element of her bail for a total of fifteen days. Add to this the thirteen days she had served since her conviction, and her net sentence left to serve was eight years and 338 days. If I have calculated it correctly, this means that she will be due for release on parole on Sunday 5 September 2032, when she will be sixty-three years old (but see 'Postscript' below).

I left the court and said farewell to a few of the reporters with whom I had become acquainted over the course of the trial. They all departed in a hurry to write their reports or do a 'piece for television' with the cameras that were now set up outside the court building. I stood in the concourse area for a while, taking it all in. It felt like my last day at school or my retirement, knowing that I was leaving for the final time and would probably never return. I thought about Teresa and how she must be feeling as she prepared for the journey back to prison, knowing that it would be her 'home' for the next nine years. I thought about Ryan and Sherri having to return to

---

[1]	The outcome of this appeal was reported on Thursday 8 February 2024. After consideration by the Solicitor General, the Attorney General's office announced that the case did not pass the required threshold and would not proceed to the Court of Appeal, adding, "The Solicitor General was saddened by this case and wishes to express his sympathies to the family of Paul Hanson."

work and having to explain to their children why Nana wouldn't be able to look after them any more. Would they move out of the area, or would they stay and endure the inevitable finger-pointing? What would become of the now notorious 21 Little London Lane?

I walked down the stairs and through the security gates. My "see yer" to the security staff was, as usual, ignored.

Postscript

Three weeks after this hearing, the court had to sit once again in order to correct an error with the sentencing. It related to the miscalculation of the credit for Teresa's time on a curfew while on bail. You would think that this could be done as an administrative amendment but, by virtue of the Criminal Justice Act 2003, it requires a formal court sitting. As per the Powers of Criminal Courts (Sentencing) Act 2000, mistakes such as this must be rectified within fifty-six days. This is commonly known as the 'Slip Rule'. It must be a regular occurrence for it to be catered for in legislation and given a nickname.

I wasn't present for this separate hearing, but it was reported that Judge Thackray was once again in charge of the virtual proceedings, with Alistair MacDonald representing the Crown and Helen Chapman standing in for Jason Pitter for the defence. The good news for the taxpayer is that Teresa wasn't required to attend the court in person. Instead, she appeared via a video link from New Hall Prison, near Wakefield. I am guessing that the hearing must have been held in Court One (which is equipped with video technology) rather than Court Four.

Anyway, the upshot was that Teresa's credit for her nightly curfews while on bail had been miscalculated by a single day. Instead of having a total deduction of fifteen days, she was now to be released sixteen days early, subject to the approval of the parole board. I am not sure that the public would consider this money well spent: a formal court sitting involving a circuit judge, two barristers and two prison officers taking up valuable court time in order to reduce the sentence of a convicted murderer by a whole day. This would mean that Teresa could now look forward to her release on Saturday 4 September 2032. However, due to the unfortunate timing of her sentencing, her nine-year term includes three leap years (2024, 2028 and 2032), so there are three February 29ths instead of the expected two. You win some, you lose some.

33

The Trial(s)

Why did it take three trials to reach a verdict? Why couldn't the jury in the first trial even reach a majority verdict after eleven hours of deliberation, but the jury in the third trial reached a unanimous verdict within three hours based on almost identical evidence? Nobody will ever know, but it is clearly a matter of luck as to who sits on the jury in each case. Their different experiences, levels of knowledge and perceptions of the evidence all play a part.

I do think, however, that if fewer shortcuts had been taken with the evidence, a verdict would have been reached in the original trial. All public services have had to make cutbacks and are still suffering a post-pandemic hangover. This means that courts are under pressure to save money and reduce the huge backlog of cases. I was surprised that the trial was listed for only five days. I can see the benefits of reducing the length of a court case: it achieves the twin aims of cutting costs and catching up with overdue cases. But the method for doing this is questionable.

Most public services and private businesses were hit hard during Covid, and relatively little work was getting done. Initially there was a total lockdown, with nobody other than essential workers allowed out. This created a huge backlog, and people had to adapt quickly. They began working from home and conducting their business over the telephone and Internet. Companies quickly realised the cost savings and continued with these arrangements. This created a legacy which now seems to have been integrated into our work culture. The courts are no different, and during lockdown cases were heard virtually, and only the witnesses who were considered essential and needed for cross-examination were required to give evidence. The rest of the evidence was paper-based and was simply read out. I would imagine the accountants couldn't believe their eyes when they compared the cost of virtual trials with live hearings. Inevitably, some of those methods will have been adopted permanently post-Covid as soon as the courts realised how much time and money could be saved.

In Teresa Hanson's final trial, only three of the ten prosecution witnesses and two of the seven defence witnesses appeared in person. The remaining twelve witnesses had their evidence agreed and their statements read out. They weren't available for cross-examination, nor for the jury to hear their live testimony or 'look them in the eyes'. The police interviews were not played in court (and very rarely are), but there was no transcript available either. I'm sure it was deemed unnecessary because Teresa's only replies were "no comment". But I believe there would have been value in reading out excerpts of the interview transcripts to show the jury the straightforward nature of the questions she had refused to answer. It would have been particularly important when she then went on to give detailed evidence in court about how the incident occurred. I think it was very fortunate for her that the judge refused to direct the jury in relation to adverse inferences, which was a surprising decision.

This explains why a murder trial was listed for only five days. Unfortunately, the court sat for a total of sixteen days in the end and required three separate trials. I can't help feeling that if the prosecution evidence had been presented in full and in person, a second and third trial might not have been necessary and proceedings would have lasted only seven or eight days rather than a total of sixteen. According to the Law Society website (based on a report published by the National Audit Office in 2017), the average cost of running a court is £2,692 per day. This figure is an average for all courts (magistrates' and Crown) but doesn't include the costs of expert witnesses, the CPS prosecutor, or the defence's legal representation (even when it is funded by legal aid). I think it would be reasonable to assume that once you have taken into account the extra expense of running a Crown Court, added the prosecution and defence costs, and allowed for inflation since 2017, you would be looking at a very conservative estimate of £5,000 per day in 2023. If this is an accurate figure, the overall cost of Teresa's three trials (which totalled fourteen days plus two half-days) would be around £75,000. If you add another day for the sentencing hearing, you would be looking at £80,000.

If all the key witnesses had appeared in the first trial and details of the police interview had been revealed, the jury might have reached a verdict. It could have saved about eight days of court time and £40,000. This may be an example of the old saying 'buy cheap and buy twice.'

The Principle of Open Justice II

With the exception of the opening day of the first trial, which was given over largely to administrative tasks, I attended every session and heard every piece of evidence in this case. I believe I was the only neutral observer to do this. Journalists and reporters cherry-picked their moments and reported sporadically. Family members were in attendance throughout but were, clearly, not impartial.

I was able to do this because of the system of open justice. This principle exists because, to paraphrase Lord Atkinson, public trials are the best means of winning public confidence and respect in justice. I didn't feel particularly welcome, although I wasn't treated with hostility either. I was certainly viewed with suspicion, and my motives were questioned by the judge, the defence barrister and the police. I was merely tolerated. I got the impression that trials being observed by neutral parties didn't happen very often. Judges and barristers will be used to reporters attending and will be familiar with most of them. Having somebody unknown to them and not connected to the case observing and taking notes was a peculiarity – a bit like wanting to witness your car's MOT test. It is an entitlement, but it is not encouraged. There are MOT viewing areas at every testing station, but most of them have probably never been used.

In the case of a murder where the defendant and the victim are not related, there would be two families affected. The victim's family would, obviously, be heartbroken and bereaved. They would want to ensure that justice was done on behalf of their loved one. A conviction and a lengthy term of imprisonment might provide them with some comfort, but it wouldn't bring back their loved one. The defendant's family, too, would be devastated. They would find it hard to believe that somebody so close to them could perpetrate such a heinous crime. If the person on trial was of good character and claimed they were not guilty, they would receive the unconditional support of their close relatives. The prospect of them serving a life sentence would be unthinkable. In both cases, they would experience anguish and financial hardship. Two families would be ruined. When the victim and the perpetrator are married only one family is affected, but with double the pain and trauma. With that, they lose all sense of objectivity.

I was largely ignored by most of Teresa's relatives, but they clearly resented me being there. I think that because the victim and the defendant were part of the same family, they thought that it was nobody else's business and they were entitled to some kind of private hearing. It's a common attitude when it comes to domestic abuse. A couple having an argument in the privacy of their own home is of no concern to outsiders. When this escalates into violence it becomes a crime and thus a public matter, which is why the police have powers of entry under such circumstances. Even then, it rarely results in a prosecution. It may not even get reported in the first place. There are usually no independent witnesses, and often, through fear, the victim will not support a criminal investigation. They may not consider themselves a victim at all. On the occasions when a victim *is* willing to provide evidence, they sometimes withdraw their complaint for pragmatic reasons. If, as a consequence of the investigation, the perpetrator loses their job and they are the main breadwinner, the victim too loses their main source of income. They may be forced to leave the family home, and their children are unlikely to want to lose their father or their mother. The victim may be pressured to drop the charges by the wider family. This is why domestic abuse is allowed to thrive and occasionally ends in a catastrophe that can't be concealed.

In a case of homicide, the victim is unable to provide a statement and has no say in the matter. But a crime is an offence against all citizens, so a defendant will be judged by their peers (the jury), and it has been this way since the Middle Ages. The state, in the form of the CPS, initiates the prosecution at public expense even without the cooperation of the victim. Murder is one of the most serious crimes of all and will inevitably attract enormous public interest.

If Paul had been killed by a stranger, the victim personal statement (VPS) given by the family would, I imagine, have described the excruciating pain he must have suffered after being stabbed and the unfairness of his life being cut short and him being deprived of a happy retirement. They would probably speak about him missing out on seeing his grandchildren grow up, and never meeting his granddaughter. He would never again be able to watch his grandsons play football or take them, with Ryan, to Elland Road to watch Leeds United. He would be unable to pursue his hobby of gardening, spend time in the hot tub or enjoy a family barbecue. He would never experience any more of the holidays he loved so much, nor would he ever drive the new car that had been ordered. His absence at future Christmas dinners would be a cruel annual reminder of the murder. I expect the family would have concluded by demanding as long a sentence as possible for the person responsible. But, sadly, in this case nobody appeared to be representing the victim. The entire family was supporting Teresa. I think the children believed that, as much as they loved their father, he couldn't be brought back, so losing their mother too was only going to make things worse. I think the family would have preferred for Paul's death to be treated as 'an accident'.

In cases of murder, the victim is unable to issue a VPS. When Ryan gave his VPS on behalf of himself and his sister, their father didn't feature in it very prominently. Ryan spoke mainly of the impact the 'accident' had had on *their* lives. He talked about losing his mother, the loss of childcare, and the time he'd had to take off work. He finished with an appeal for leniency. But the relationship between the victim and the perpetrator should be irrelevant. A prosecution wasn't in the family's interest, but it was in the *public* interest. This is why objectivity is required in the form of a state-sponsored prosecution, a judge, a jury, and an open system of justice in which journalists are free to witness proceedings and report back to the public and the public (like me) are free to come and see for themselves. It keeps things honest and transparent. In this case, we had the rare situation of a murder trial in which the victim's immediate family were not supporting the prosecution.

Teresa offered a guilty plea to the lesser charge of manslaughter which, had it been accepted, would have removed the need for an expensive jury trial and would have resulted in a much lighter sentence. In February 2024 there was a huge backlog of 64,000 cases in the Crown Court system (according to HM Courts data). In October 2023 UK prisons had a combined population of 88,000, according to government figures, and were full. The government were actively seeking ways to reduce both problems. You might ask: where is the incentive for the state to go ahead with an expensive prosecution which, if successful, would lead to a very lengthy and expensive stay in prison for a middle-aged woman who nobody believes is a danger to the public? If the state could save the taxpayer a small fortune and minimise the heartache and devastation of the family without endangering the public, why couldn't they accept a manslaughter charge? It's in everyone's interests, surely? From where does the motivation come for a very expensive trial and an even more costly prison sentence?

Step forward the CPS, who are independent of the judiciary, the government and the police. At the end of an initial police investigation, the CPS decides with what offence, if any, the suspect is charged. Once the full investigation is complete, they have a two-stage test to decide whether or not to prosecute. It is called the Code for Crown Prosecutors, and the CPS will only pursue a charge if both tests are satisfied:

1.   There is sufficient evidence to provide a realistic prospect of conviction.
2.   The prosecution is in the public interest.

Note: test two says that a prosecution must be in the *public* interest. Not the government's, not the victim's and not the police's.

Until 1986, it was the responsibility of the police not only to investigate crime but also to decide whether to charge and prosecute suspects. This caused a potential conflict of interest, and investigators, under pressure from the public, would sometimes identify and charge the wrong person, which could then lead to a miscarriage of justice. The Stefan Kiszko case in 1976 is a particularly shocking example. Thankfully, we now have a system in which the victims, the investigators, the prosecutors and the judiciary are all independent of the government (and each other), and, apart from the victims, they are all fully accountable.

We have seen recently, with the Post Office scandal, how things can go spectacularly wrong without these safeguards. There may be questionable motives if the alleged victim of a crime (in this case the Post Office, which is wholly owned by the government) goes on to carry out their own investigation and prosecution. Such motives are very rarely in the public interest or in the interest of justice. In Teresa's case, the CPS decided that there was sufficient evidence for a realistic prospect of a conviction for murder, and she was therefore charged with that offence. If there had been any justification in law for her actions (such as being a victim of domestic abuse, and/or a loss of control), the prosecution might have accepted her offer to plead guilty to manslaughter. The decision to prosecute her for murder may not have been in the family's interest, but the CPS decided that it was in the *public* interest.

Teresa insisted that the stabbing was a complete accident. She hoped to convince a jury of this, be found not guilty, and just walk free. Unfortunately, there was no credible evidence to suggest that it was an accident, so Alistair MacDonald, on behalf of the CPS, said that there was "no basis" for accepting a manslaughter plea: "I have my instructions and the trial must go ahead." The murder trial went ahead as planned, and so the outcome was taken out of the hands of the judge and barristers and handed to a jury – twelve members of the public, in whose interest the prosecution was brought in the first place. In the original trial, the jury came close to returning an alternative verdict of manslaughter or even acquitting Teresa altogether. As we know, at the third time of asking she was quickly found guilty of murder on clear evidence and was convicted and later sentenced. The jury weren't swayed by the emotion of it all and certainly weren't convinced by her defence.

As my account of the events suggests, the conviction of Teresa Hanson wasn't a straightforward journey but took a long, clunky, expensive and circuitous route to eventually come to a conclusion. It was rather like using an out-of-date satnav which you occasionally ignore, taking a shortcut and getting lost before eventually arriving at your destination. You get there in the end. But what if the CPS had taken the easy way out and accepted a guilty plea? There would have been no trial and no jury. Would anyone ever know? Would anyone care? I like to think that the answer to both of these questions is yes, but how does the public hold the CPS to account?

This case, like most murder cases, attracted a lot of public interest. This interest is generated mostly by reading about an incident online or watching the news on television. The reporters are usually alerted by members of the public, who have seen a great deal of police activity and want to know what's going on. The police are accountable to the public and so will issue statements and give interviews to journalists and reporters, and they often appeal to the public for information. The story is followed to its conclusion by reporters, normally when someone is charged. Up until that point, the police are often quite reticent with regard to the details, for operational and legal reasons. It isn't until the case reaches court for trial or sentencing that the (almost) full details are revealed. The reporters are always going to attend to hear the 'juicy' details, because (if you want to be cynical) these attract viewers and sell papers. However, reporters aren't stupid, and they will soon know or find out if anything improper or underhand goes on. The journalist Nick Wallis had spent years reporting on the Post Office scandal, with little public or government interest. It took a television drama to ignite people's outrage and bring about any meaningful action.

Then you get oddballs like me who simply wander into the court, without warning, to see what's going on. You don't need a ticket; you don't have to reveal your identity, give advance warning or explain yourself; you can just turn up and watch for free. It may have caused a bit of consternation, but I have that right. I am not a reporter, a legal expert or a member of the family. I am a citizen, a taxpayer and a member of the public and, therefore, an interested party. Before the trial began, I never planned to write a book, but I was able to do so because of the system of open justice.

35

Domestic Abuse

So how did it come to this? These are the devastating consequences of a moment of madness or a flash of temper. All logical thinking is temporarily suspended when the red mist descends and violence takes over. This is why preventive laws exist: to try to avoid the circumstances which frequently lead to violence.

Under the Public Order Act 1986 it is an offence to use threatening or abusive words that may provoke violence, but the Act makes a specific exception where both parties are in a private dwelling. The Criminal Justice Act 1988 makes it an offence to possess any article with a blade or a sharp point unless you have a good excuse, but this too only applies if you are in a public place. Clearly, these laws are intended to prevent violence on the street. Most stabbings involve young people and are often gang-related or fuelled by alcohol. In a public place the police can use their stop and search powers to seize weapons and arrest offenders before violence occurs. Of course you will never stop violence altogether, but a mere fist fight usually results in just a few bumps and bruises, which most people put down to alcohol-induced behaviour.

None of this applies in the domestic setting, where there can be an abundance of knives and other potential weapons close to hand. Unfortunately, when an argument gets out of hand between partners in the privacy of their own home, there may be no one else there to witness it or to intervene and prevent it escalating into violence. Red wine and red mist, combined with the ready availability of knives, can make a lethal cocktail, as we saw in this case.

The statutory definition for domestic abuse includes violent or threatening behaviour between people aged sixteen or over who are "personally connected". The case of Teresa Hanson would, obviously, be recorded as a domestic abuse incident. According to Home Office figures collated for the three years between April 2019 and March 2022, there were 370 domestic homicides in England and Wales. Of these, only thirty (8.1%) involved a male victim whose female partner was the alleged perpetrator. The Office for National Statistics tells us that in the same period, only 17% of all females convicted of homicide (not just domestic homicide) were aged forty-five to fifty-four. This, combined with the earlier figures, would suggest that the number of women in this age group convicted of killing their male partner in England and Wales could be as few as five over a three-year period.

A 2020 report by the Australian Institute of Criminology, *Female perpetrated intimate partner homicide: Indigenous and non-Indigenous offenders*, states: "research has found that women who kill their intimate partners are, on average, older…and more likely to be married, have children and be cohabiting with the victim… than other female homicide offenders." The report also says: "The most common motive for female perpetrated IPH [intimate partner homicide] was an argument of a domestic nature [57% of cases]." Apart from infidelity, the most common type of dispute in these kinds of incident was an argument about alcohol consumption.

Although statistically this type of case is very rare, the version of events put forward by Teresa is even rarer. In fact, it might even be non-existent. Teresa gave evidence on oath to say that the stabbing was purely accidental. The testimony of the forensic pathologist, Dr Michael Parsons, included research which, coincidentally, was carried out in Australia and examined 1,136 cases of death caused by a sharp instrument such as a knife. In this study, there were no cases of an accidental single stab wound. Despite the lack of empirical evidence, Dr Parsons did say that it was theoretically possible to accidentally stab somebody with a lightly gripped knife, but also that it was "highly unlikely". In his closing speech the defence counsel Alistair MacDonald continued the theme, saying: "It is theoretically possible, but nobody can say there won't ever be a case of a plane crashing in Leeds city centre. There are millions of flights in and out of Leeds Bradford Airport every year, but it has never happened." (It may be worth adding that shortly after the trial, on Friday 20 October 2023, a plane skidded off the runway at Leeds Bradford Airport while attempting to land in heavy rain, causing the airport to close.) Everything that happens for the first time has never happened before.

Domestic abuse is known to increase in frequency and severity over time. The statutory definition includes psychological and emotional abuse. Teresa herself said in her prepared statement at the police station that "over the years, my husband has been verbally and mentally abusive to me." This wasn't said without thinking; this was a signed written statement, made after due consideration and following the advice of a qualified legal representative. So we can be sure that there were previous occasions of Paul verbally abusing his wife. This often occurs following excessive drinking, as on the day of the incident. We know from neighbours and from Teresa herself that alcohol was a prominent feature in both their lives. She even admitted that Paul was prone to "secret drinking". What we don't know is if any of these previous incidents had been reported to the police. It's not uncommon for victims to cover up signs of abuse and refuse to admit that any kind of incident has occurred, out of shame or fear of retribution. We can never be sure what goes on behind closed doors. Prior to this appalling incident, had the police ever had cause to visit 21 Little London Lane following reports of domestic discord? It may be that neighbours reported previous incidents. When the police receive a report of a domestic incident (not necessarily a crime) it must be recorded, even if it appears unfounded and both parties deny that any incident has taken place. I don't know if Paul was of good character or if the police had ever recorded any previous incidents at the Hansons' address.

I was curious to know what was behind Judge Thackray's comments at the sentencing hearing. In his judgment, he praised Teresa for seeking to protect her husband's reputation by playing down his aggressive behaviour. To what was he referring? She had made a statement saying that she had suffered years of verbal and mental abuse, and had given evidence that on the night, Paul had called her "a bitch" and had shouted at her to chuck the tea "in the fucking bin". If this is playing down his aggressive behaviour, what other information is there that wasn't mentioned in court?

36

Teresa Hanson's Evidence

From the outset, Teresa's defence was completely absurd and doomed to failure. I can't understand how she was allowed to put forward such a weak and confusing defence.

Everybody who is arrested by the police and detained at a police station is entitled to free legal advice, funded by the legal aid scheme. Under the Criminal Legal Aid (Remuneration) Regulations 2013 (as amended), a 'duty solicitor' attending a police station in Hull (as at January 2024) can claim an 'all-in' fixed fee of £176.30 in legal aid. If the case passes a certain threshold, they are able to claim an hourly rate. It is a very complicated system in which the hourly rate varies according to the location, the time of day and the seriousness of the offence. Theoretically, a solicitor could spend up to eight hours assisting an arrested person before exceeding the threshold, and their employers could still only claim the fixed fee. That would work out at £22 per hour. From this amount, the firm of solicitors would have to pay them their salary (sometimes enhanced for working unsocial hours), a callout fee, travelling expenses and possibly a meal allowance. In addition, they still have their overheads in terms of administrative staff, rent, heating and lighting, etc. Knowing that police station representation is unlikely to be profitable, firms of solicitors see it as a gateway to more lucrative business but are keen to keep their costs to a minimum. I suspect this is why, late at night in the busy Christmas period, the firm concerned chose to send an accredited legal representative to represent Teresa (facing a murder charge) rather than a fully qualified solicitor. To quote from the website of Old Bailey Solicitors, the fixed fee system:

> *does not always mean that the client receives the highest standard of care. In fairness, the system is not designed, and is certainly not funded, so as to provide the very highest of standards.*

In her first interview, which was before any meaningful police evidence was disclosed to her, Teresa chose, on the advice of her legal representative, to make a prepared statement. It is not known if the *contents* of that statement were approved by her legal representative or whether she went against her advice. In the first part she stated: "Over the years, my husband has been verbally and mentally abusive to me." This would suggest that she had been a long-term victim of domestic abuse. The only reasons to bring this up (shortly after learning of Paul's death) would be to offer some justification for her actions and as a precursor for a claim of self-defence or provocation. It is also, in my opinion, a tacit admission that her actions were deliberate. This was immediately followed by the second part of her prepared statement, in which she said: "The injury occurred whilst I was holding the knife when he walked onto it. At no time did I intend to kill him or cause him serious harm." Apart from the ludicrous claim that her husband had simply walked onto the knife she was holding (an excuse on a par with 'the dog ate my homework'), this appears contradictory to the first part of the statement, in that she was now saying that the fatal injury was a complete accident. You are compelled to ask, 'Which is it? If the first part is true, why not pursue your claim of self-defence? If the second part is true, why is the first part relevant?' She appeared to be backing two horses.

During her three interviews, the police sought to clarify her statement and to resolve the many unanswered questions. The most obvious is: why was she holding a knife in the first place? Unfortunately, these questions remained unanswered as, on legal advice, Teresa responded with "no comment" to any request for even the most basic information. She would have had numerous consultations with her accredited legal representative at various stages of her detention, and I wonder what advice she received. Was she badly advised, or did she receive sound advice that she chose to ignore? We shall never know, because legal advice is subject to legal privilege. Although legal privilege is sacrosanct, there appears to be an exception if it can help your case. Having given your detailed evidence in court, when you are asked why you failed to offer an explanation to the police, you can simply say 'I was advised not to by my legal representative, and it never crossed my mind to ignore the legal advice.'

After Teresa was charged, she pleaded not guilty and was eventually bailed. Her firm of solicitors will have instructed a barrister to prepare her case and to represent her in the subsequent trial. The hearing was scheduled for 12 June 2023, and the CPS were then obliged to disclose the prosecution evidence to the defence. In return, the defence team were required to provide their defence statement, which we now know was revealed on 31 May 2023 – only twelve days before the trial.

Having had the benefit of studying the evidence put forward by the prosecution (which slightly undermined the prepared statement given at the police station), the defence team offered a rather different explanation for Paul's death. The previously alleged verbal and mental abuse seemed to have dropped off the agenda. This was, presumably, in response to the statement of Ryan Hanson, who said he didn't remember a "cross word" between his parents and had never witnessed any arguments or bickering. The defence team would also have read the report and statement of the forensic pathologist, Dr Michael Parsons, which gave details about the stab wound. Specifically, he said that it was 129 centimetres (four feet three inches) from the heel of Paul's foot and that it was "highly unlikely" that it had been caused by him walking onto a lightly gripped knife. Had Teresa stuck to her original story – that Paul had simply walked onto the knife – she would have had to explain why she was holding the knife at shoulder height. This required a modification to her original account, in that she was now claiming in her revised statement that the accidental stabbing had occurred while she was chopping onions when she tried to push Paul away, forgetting that she had a knife in her hand. In an attempt to explain how the onions were cooked when the police arrived, she also added that she didn't realise until "afterwards" that he was injured.

Curiously, during the 999 calls made immediately after the event, there was no mention of chopping onions or pushing her husband away. Even in her prepared statement at the police station, made after she'd had time to gather her thoughts, there were still no references to these critical events. It must have slipped her memory. Most significantly, there was no mention of the delay in noticing his injury and subsequent collapse. Maybe this was because her memory had been refreshed once she had seen the police evidence stating that, on their arrival, the onions had been cooked and the hob was turned off. Perhaps she had overlooked these facts during her stay at the police station because she was so distraught. It was fortunate that she was able to remember all of these details just before the deadline for submitting a defence statement.

The first opportunity for the prosecution to put Teresa's evidence to the test would happen during the trial at Hull Crown Court. The defendant can't be compelled to give evidence, but under the circumstances she had little choice. In her evidence in chief, she claimed that she and Paul had had an argument about his drinking while she was preparing tea. This went on for about ten minutes until he walked off and slammed the door. He then returned to the kitchen and became abusive. She told the court that she was chopping onions with a small kitchen knife when she turned to push him away, forgetting that she was still holding the knife. She said, under oath, that he had simply walked off and she had thought that that was the end of the matter. Meanwhile, she finished chopping the onions and rolled some pastry before placing the onions in the pan to cook and caramelise them. After about ten minutes, she had finished cooking the onions and was disturbed by the sound of her dog barking. It was only on investigating this that she saw her husband lying on the dining room floor in a large pool of blood. She had no idea what had happened until she saw where the blood was coming from and then realised that she must have stabbed him by accident.

There are numerous problems with this account. Some were dealt with during her cross-examination and some weren't. For the sake of simplicity, I have listed them below:

1. Teresa claimed that the door was slammed only once before she accidentally stabbed Paul. The next-door neighbour, Shaun Trafford, said he heard the "banging and slamming of internal doors" for a period of ten minutes before it suddenly went quiet. We were told that Paul was standing at the open back door enjoying a cigarette before the argument started, but that door was locked when the ambulance crew arrived. Who locked it and why?

2. Teresa said in her evidence that the time between the accidental stabbing and finding Paul in a pool of blood was, coincidentally, about ten minutes. In that time, she claimed she cooked the onions she had been chopping. The BBC's 'Good Food' website says that caramelising onions takes thirty-five to forty-five minutes. When the police arrived, the onions had been cooked and the hob was turned off.

3. Teresa swore on oath that the accidental stabbing occurred when Paul returned to the kitchen being

abusive, at which point she turned and pushed him away, forgetting that she was holding a knife. She even gave a physical demonstration of this manoeuvre in court. Assuming she was holding the knife in the way it would normally be held to chop vegetables, it is very difficult to imagine how she could push him away and accidentally stab him at the angle at which the blade entered his body and with sufficient force to penetrate his heart and aorta.

4. Teresa told the court that Paul had been coming towards her shouting abuse, she accidentally stabbed him, and he then simply turned around and walked off without saying or doing anything out of the ordinary. She didn't think it odd that pushing him away instantly ended his abusive behaviour and caused him to retreat without a reaction. Furthermore, she didn't see him bent double before collapsing to the floor just a few metres away, or see the trail of blood which began a few feet away after he had, in the words of Dr Parsons, suffered "profuse" bleeding.

5. We were told by the forensic pathologist that the "external bleeding would have started rapidly", and yet the blood on the kitchen floor was only a few feet away from where Teresa was chopping onions. Did Paul stagger backwards before the bleeding began or was he stabbed in the place where the blood was found (which was some distance away from the chopping board)? If it was the latter, then her account of turning around to push him while chopping onions doesn't really stack up.

6. Following the accidental stabbing, Teresa was completely oblivious to her husband's plight – so

much so that she continued chopping the onions with the same knife that had entered his body to a depth of 8.5 centimetres (3.5 inches) and she failed to notice that it was now covered in blood and fatty deposits. I would think that, even for an expert, chopping vegetables with a sharp knife requires a high level of concentration. Not only that, but the blood and fatty deposits had, apparently, remained on the blade after she finished chopping the onions. In the report from the forensic scientist, there was no mention of any trace of onion on the blade.

7. Teresa would have us believe that while Paul was lying on the (open-plan) dining room floor just a few metres away, bleeding profusely, she was able to finish chopping the onions, place them in a preheated pan, cook them until they were caramelised, and turn off the hob. Not only that, but she managed to roll out the pastry while the onions were cooking – and do all of this within ten minutes, totally unaware of her husband's predicament.

8. According to her evidence, Teresa became aware that something was amiss only when she was alerted by her dog barking. The statements from her next-door neighbours made no mention of hearing a dog bark. We weren't told the whereabouts of Kiki before, during or immediately after the incident. It seems that Kiki wasn't perturbed by the loud, lengthy and heated argument between her owners and only became anxious some ten minutes after Paul fell to the floor bleeding heavily. Yet, as far as I know, there were no paw prints in the blood where Kiki had allegedly been standing and barking. A dog's sense of smell is far more powerful than a human's. This may

be speculative, but most dogs I know would always be in the vicinity where food is being prepared. Second, even if Kiki was somehow unaware of her owners' altercation (she may be deaf), I would have thought that the smell of blood would have attracted her attention. Apparently not. Wherever she was hiding beforehand, she decided to take a stroll through the house ten minutes after the commotion had subsided. Then, by pure chance, she came across Paul lying on the floor in a pool of blood with his legs bent awkwardly underneath him, and realised that something wasn't quite right. She decided to alert Teresa (standing only five metres away) to her husband's situation, and at this point must have considered her task to be complete, judging by the lack of barking in the background of the 999 call.

9. During the second 999 call, Teresa did say that she had stabbed Paul accidentally, but the full sentence was "I was cooking tea, we had an argument, and I accidentally stabbed him." Note that she said "cooking tea", not 'preparing tea' or 'chopping onions'. Maybe this is a bit harsh and what she said was not meant literally, but I think it is safe to assume that the onions were already cooked when she made the phone call at 7.05pm. Having discovered Paul lying in a pool of blood, there are two options relating to how and when she turned off the cooker:

   a. It was merely a coincidence that Kiki barked immediately after Teresa turned off the cooker, having finished cooking the onions.

   b. Teresa was still cooking the onions when Kiki interrupted her. She noticed Paul lying in a pool of blood but still had the presence of mind to turn off the cooker before going to his aid, and it was a pure coincidence that the onions were cooked perfectly at this point.

Following the 'accidental stabbing', I think we can allow Teresa a couple of minutes to finish chopping the onions before cooking them. According to her, it then took a further ten minutes to actually cook and caramelise the onions. I would then estimate that at least a few minutes were required to discover Paul's injuries, go to his aid and call the ambulance. Even by Teresa's questionable timings, and being on the generous side, this would total at the very least fifteen minutes. Unfortunately, three minutes into her first 999 call at 7.08pm, Teresa was asked when the stabbing had occurred and she replied, "About five minutes ago." This works out at 7.03pm, only two minutes before the call was made. This would also coincide with the time she claims she was "cooking tea" and first realised her husband was injured. Based on her version of events, she "pushed him away" at about 6.50pm, some eighteen minutes previously. Of course, five minutes is a rough estimate, but eighteen minutes is quite a difference.

I have put together a timeline of the events, starting with the time Teresa made the statement during the 999 call that it happened "about five minutes ago" (7.08pm), which is indisputable. I have then used her testimony of the timings to work backwards to the point when the argument began, which indicates a time of approximately 6.40pm.

See the table opposite…

Action	Real time	Duration
Argument begins.	6.40pm	10 minutes
Argument ends, door is slammed, and Paul retreats while Teresa resumes chopping onions.	6.50pm	0 minutes
Paul returns to the kitchen and is 'pushed away' (stabbed) by Teresa.	6.50pm	2 minutes
Teresa cooks and caramelises onions.	6.52pm	10 minutes
After hearing the dog bark, Teresa discovers her husband on the dining room floor and checks him out before calling an ambulance.	7.02pm	3 minutes
First 999 call.	7.05pm	3 minutes
999 call statement that the stabbing happened "about five minutes ago".	7.08pm	

Teresa and Paul in happier times

(Enterprise News & Pictures)

Paul Hanson pictured at home with a bottle of wine and their dog

(Enterprise News & Pictures)

37

What Really Happened?

This is the question to which everybody would like to know the answer. The only person who can tell us is Teresa Hanson. If, like, the jury, you did not believe Teresa's testimony, we may never find out the truth, because, astonishingly, the parole board can release her on licence in 2032 without an admission, an explanation or even an expression of remorse. After nine years, long after her case is forgotten, I expect she will be quietly released back into the community to resume her relationship with her family, and the public will be none the wiser.

The only incentive for her to tell the truth would be to clear her conscience. There may be a problem with that, because her son and daughter, at least, seem to believe her claim that the death of their father was a complete accident. Even after her conviction for murder, Ryan referred to "the accident" in his VPS. I honestly can't make up my mind as to whether he and Sherri truly believed her evidence or were toeing the party line in a show of loyalty and support for their mother. It is one thing for objective observers like me or members of the jury to decide. When it's your own mother, you lack that objectivity and *want* to believe her account.

I have to say, Teresa did better than I expected in the witness box. Barristers can't represent you if you admit the offence to them but then deny it in court. They are not permitted to 'coach' their clients either, but I am sure that Jason Pitter discussed with her the types of questions she was likely to be asked. She probably went through the imaginary scenario many times in her mind, blotting out the unpalatable truth. Based on her account, she will have identified the gaps in her story and anticipated the questions she would be likely to face during the cross-examination, constructing and possibly rehearsing her answers. She had staked her future on this account, and so will have gone over it multiple times, practising it until it was fixed in her memory.

They say that to be a convincing liar, you have to believe the story yourself. This may explain Teresa's better-than-expected performance. To quote the novelist Mark Lawrence:

I'm a good liar. A great one. And to be a great liar you have to live your lies, to believe them, to the point that when you tell them to yourself enough times, even what's right before your eyes will bend itself to the falsehood.

I think Teresa was so shocked by what had happened that she could not bring herself to believe the truth. It was clearly a flash of temper and an overreaction, with fatal consequences. It was a huge mistake which she immediately regretted but was unable to rectify. She was desperate and, in a childlike response, she slapped Paul's face, telling him to wake up, unaware of the severity of his injuries. Soon the gravity of the situation and the possible consequences began to dawn on her and so, in her despair, she offered the ambulance crew £1,000 to save him. They could not save him, so when the nightmare was confirmed and she was told that Paul had died, she couldn't face the reality or the responsibility. Her husband, her childhood sweetheart, her partner of thirty-seven years was dead, and she had killed him. It was a fact she couldn't admit to herself, let alone anybody else.

The sad thing is that had she told the whole truth (or what I believe to be the truth), she might well have faced the lesser charge of manslaughter. She might have been treated leniently by Judge Thackray, who was clearly sympathetic to her situation. On a charge of murder, the life sentence is fixed by law. For manslaughter, the judge has wider discretion and can reduce the sentence by up to one-third for an early guilty plea. Even if she'd faced a prison sentence of nine years for manslaughter, this could have been reduced to six years for pleading guilty. Also, unlike the sentence for murder, for manslaughter the offender receives a 'determinate sentence', which requires only half the sentence to be served in custody and the remainder on licence. It is possible, therefore, that had she been completely honest from the start, she could have served a mere three years in custody and would have been eligible for release as early as 2026. Nobody believes that she intended to kill Paul, and she may not even have intended to cause him serious harm, but the jury decided she did deliberately stab him. Alas, she couldn't bring herself to accept that simple truth. She knew what she had done but convinced herself that, rather than being a mistake, it was an accident. An accident was easier for her to square with her conscience, and it mitigated her culpability. Maybe she feared that telling the truth would mean being shunned by her family. Perhaps facing a murder conviction was preferable to a lighter sentence and being ostracised by her children. She had lost her husband; her children were all she had left. If they believed it was an accident, they might stand by her. And so began the lie.

Although her testimony was delivered in a convincing manner, its content did not stand up to scrutiny, and it didn't help that she was forced to revise her account in the face of the prosecution evidence. There were no direct witnesses to what had happened, but the scientific and medical evidence was overwhelming.

If this wasn't enough to persuade the jury, the 999 calls should have removed any doubt. These were made before Teresa realised that Paul had suffered fatal injuries, before she was aware of the fatal outcome, and before receiving any legal advice. Her comments in the first call sought to minimise what had happened but were largely true. By the time the second call was made, she'd done a bit of thinking and it had become "an accident". Having unexpectedly been put through to the police, she appeared to adopt a tone of hostility. She said she didn't think their attendance was necessary, but then said, "You can come if you like." When informed the police were on their way, she responded with an almost sarcastic "Yeah, fine." In her earlier comment to the police she came very close to a confession. She said, "He told me to fuck off and called me a bitch so I…I don't know what I did." I think she stopped herself before saying, 'so I stabbed him', and hesitated before replacing it with "I don't know what I did."

At the risk of overanalysing this sentence and reading too much into it, I considered the importance of the word 'so'. This simple two-letter word linked the verbal abuse she received with the stabbing. In other words, they weren't two separate events, as she later claimed: the stabbing was a consequence of the abuse. Used as a conjunction (as in this case), the *Cambridge Dictionary* defines 'so' as "and for that reason; therefore". So (intentional use) Teresa's comment could be interpreted as 'He told me to fuck off and called me a bitch, and for that reason I stabbed him.'

I very much doubt that the jury analysed the evidence this deeply. They didn't need to. I've had months to go through it, and they required only a few hours to return their guilty verdict.

38

A Reconstruction

I have pieced together an account of what I believe happened on the evening of Wednesday 28 December 2022. Based on all the evidence, including sections of Teresa's testimony I accept as truthful, I have compiled the following:

The relationship between Paul and Teresa Hanson was, generally, a happy and stable one. They were planning for the future, as evidenced by them booking a holiday and ordering a new car. Paul's behaviour had become more challenging following his brain injury and was exacerbated by his drinking. I imagine this became worse over time as his drinking increased and became excessive. His excessive and 'secret' drinking caused him to be aggressive towards his wife, especially when challenged. This would occasionally develop into a heated argument, as witnessed from time to time by their neighbours. The aggression could sometimes turn into bullying and abuse. This was confirmed by Teresa herself stating that she had suffered years of verbal and mental abuse.

It was only three days after Christmas, and the Hansons hoped to relax and take things easy. They had visited Teresa's sister-in-law to deliver her birthday present, and had been to the local supermarket to get something for tea. They had planned a quiet and relaxed night in on their own and, on returning home, Teresa put on some music before gathering the ingredients for their evening meal of Mediterranean tart. Drink was integral in both their lives, so while the meal was being prepared a bottle of Rioja was opened and they began drinking. They were relaxed and happy and even had a dance together.

At about 6.15pm Teresa began preparing the meal by chopping the onions and rolling the pastry. At about 6.20pm she placed the onions in the preheated pan to cook and caramelise them, ready for 7pm. The small kitchen knife she used to chop the onions was probably left on the chopping board on the kitchen surface. While she was cooking the onions, Paul came into the kitchen in a happy mood, singing along to the music. He opened the back door, lit a cigarette and helped himself to his fourth glass of wine. It was about 6.45pm and Teresa noticed that he was a little worse for wear. She knew that he had a habit of drinking to excess before falling asleep on the sofa. She had gone to a lot of trouble making the tea, and didn't want the evening spoiled and the meal to go to waste. So she challenged him, suggesting that he'd had enough, and asked him not to drink any more until after tea.

To use Teresa's own phrase, Paul then "clicked". He responded aggressively by shouting at her, "Shut up, you bitch, don't tell me what to do. I can drink what I like!"

Teresa, who'd had a couple of glasses of wine herself, was understandably upset by this behaviour and shouted back, "Don't you speak to me like that!" and things escalated.

Paul responded by banging the back door shut and walking off into the living room, slamming the door behind him. Still seething, he then returned to the kitchen, slamming the door shut once again and shouting, "I don't want tea, chuck it in the fucking bin!" before walking back into the living room and again closing the door forcefully. This would explain their neighbour Shaun Trafford's account of internal doors being slammed for ten minutes.

Teresa, who was obviously angry and upset and possibly in tears, continued cooking the tea. By now the onions were cooked and caramelised, so she turned off the hob. The pastry was rolled and tea was almost ready. It was 7pm, and she hoped that Paul had calmed down and was ready for his evening meal. Instead, he'd drunk even more wine, so when she shouted to him that his tea was ready, he stormed out of the living room in a rage. Slamming the door yet again, he walked into the kitchen, shouting aggressively, "I told you, I don't want tea, chuck it in the fucking bin!" He was walking towards her with the intention of putting the contents of the pan straight into the bin.

Teresa attempted to stop him by standing in his way and trying to push him back. She was overpowered by her much stronger husband, who was intent on throwing away the meal that she had spent so long preparing. Overwhelmed by anger and frustration, and following a struggle, she snapped and lost control. She picked up the knife from the chopping board and plunged the blade into his chest, quickly withdrawing it as she came to her senses and realised what she'd done. Paul bent over in pain and staggered backwards as he began to bleed heavily. This left a trail of blood on the kitchen floor as he retreated and eventually collapsed on the dining room floor, his legs bent awkwardly underneath him. As her husband lay there, gurgling and with blood pouring from his chest, Teresa was in shock, not believing what had just happened. After putting the knife back on the surface, still covered in blood and fatty deposits, she went to his assistance. Recognising the gravity of the situation and still in a panic, she picked up her phone and dialled 999.

Following her arrest she had convinced herself that it was an accident, so she told the police that Paul had walked onto the knife. She couldn't deny killing him, but she did deny that it was a deliberate act and denied any intention to cause harm.

She was later confronted with the prosecution evidence and needed to explain what she was doing with the knife and why she had been holding it at shoulder height. She then invented the story of chopping onions and 'pushing him away'. When it was pointed out that the onions had already been cooked, she came up with the preposterous explanation of cooking them after the stabbing, unaware of what had happened. This didn't explain how she had failed to notice the presence of blood and fatty deposits on the knife, how those contaminants remained in place even after the knife was used to finish chopping the onions, or the disappearance of thirty minutes from the timeline.

This, in my opinion, was her undoing. It was a lie too far. Up until then, she was actually telling half-truths. He *did* walk towards her – but not onto the knife. She *did* push him away – but not with the knife in her hand. She *was* using the knife to chop onions – but forty minutes earlier. The jury didn't believe it, and neither did I.

> *You can fool all the people some of the time and some of*
> *the people all the time, but you cannot fool all the people*
> *all the time.*
> (Commonly attributed to Abraham Lincoln)

> *Oh, what a tangled web we weave, when first we practise*
> *to deceive.*
> (Sir Walter Scott)

The simple truth can be found in Teresa's opening remark in her first 999 call: "We had an argument and I stabbed him – just out of anger. We was having a row."

39

The Future

New Hall Prison is located near the village of Flockton in West Yorkshire, not far from junction 39 of the M1 and about a forty-five-minute drive from Goole. It is a prison and young offender institution which accommodates women over the age of eighteen, and it is where Teresa Hanson will reside until at least 2032. I suppose she is lucky that her family live relatively close by and will be able to visit regularly.

As I write this (1 January 2024), Teresa is turning fifty-five, on her second birthday spent in custody. I wonder what kind of Christmas she and her family have had. Christmas 2022 was hosted by Paul and Teresa at 21 Little London Lane, with their children and grandchildren and Teresa's parents all in attendance. It was described by their daughter, Sherri, as "the best day today with family". Christmas 2023 will have been very different. Did the remaining family gather together, and if so, who hosted the event? Were Ryan and Sherri able to celebrate the occasion without their mother and father? Did they put on a brave face for the sake of their young children? Under the circumstances, can they allow themselves to smile and enjoy life – not just at Christmas but at any time? One thing is certain: the Christmas holidays will never be the same again for the Hanson family. And how did Teresa spend Christmas and her birthday? Prison rules don't allow incoming phone calls and don't permit visits on bank holidays, so nobody could call or visit her on

Christmas Day or her birthday. Maybe she was able to speak briefly to some of her relatives on the telephone, but she will have spent most of her time on these important dates in her cell or associating with the other inmates.

What of 28 December 2023, a year on from the 'accident'? It was, of course, the anniversary of Paul's passing. Did Teresa or the family mark it in any way, or was it much too painful to even think about? As well as losing her husband of thirty-three years, Teresa will now have minimal contact with her relatives. For such a close family, this must be heartbreaking. She will miss her grandsons terribly and will have had very little time to get acquainted with her baby granddaughter. I would think it is a difficult decision whether or not to take young children to visit their grandmother in prison. How on earth do you explain to children of that age about the death of their grandfather and why their grandmother is no longer around?

On Teresa's release, her eldest grandchildren will practically be adults, and will almost certainly ask lots of questions and eventually do their own research. Even if they don't, I'm sure there will be plenty of people with long memories who will be all too keen to fill them in on the details. In circumstances like this, people sometimes move out of the area to avoid gossip and finger-pointing, but that would be very disruptive for the young children. Ryan and Sherri both work locally, so moving away would be a big upheaval for them too. Although their mother is no longer available to do school runs or perform childcare duties, they have a large extended family and numerous close friends who may be able to assist. Moving away would mean no family, no friends, and very expensive childcare. On the positive side, Teresa will be only sixty-three years of age when she regains her freedom. In the interim she will, I'm sure, receive regular visits and phone calls from her grandchildren and watch them grow up and reach their milestones. She will, no doubt, receive lots of letters from them and have photos and samples of their schoolwork on her cell walls.

Although it may not be something she will be concerned about at the moment, Teresa will eventually have to plan for her future beyond her prison release. If her house has been sold she will be entitled to the proceeds, and ordinarily the financial hardship caused by the unexpected death of a spouse would be cushioned by a life insurance payout or the receipt of a portion of their occupational pension. I don't know if Paul's life was insured or even if Teresa was the beneficiary, but if so, as she was convicted of his murder the insurers will not be paying her out on the policy. If Paul contributed to a workplace pension scheme I would be surprised if, under the circumstances, Teresa is entitled to receive payments from it. I am sure that she will be welcomed back into the family on her release and will be offered accommodation at her parents' house, where she lived while on bail. Sadly, she will probably leave prison with no home of her own, no job and (given her age) no pension until 2036.

The final word, however, should be reserved for the victim. Having lost his father at a young age, Paul Hanson survived a near-fatal road accident at the age of twenty-nine. Thirteen years later, aged forty-two, he required neurosurgery following a serious assault at his local pub. His luck finally ran out in 2022 when he was stabbed to death in his own home at the age of just fifty-four. What a cruel and tragic irony that the person who had stood loyally by him, cared for him lovingly and nursed him through these challenging times was the one responsible for ending his life: his own wife.

Acknowledgements

Like a lot of people, I often thought about writing a book as I have always been interested in language and writing – although my old English teacher would probably disagree.

The trouble is, I never really knew what to write about. I'd had a long and exciting career in the police with enough material to fill several books – but it's all been done before. With the current proliferation of 'real life' police programmes on TV, a book about my modest career would be unlikely to create much interest – and novels just aren't my thing.

I have always enjoyed reading non-fiction, particularly the autobiographies of people who inspire me, and true-crime stories. I suppose it is really all about people; what drives them to achieve success and motivates them to commit serious crime?

I came to the conclusion that having no subject matter and insufficient time, writing a book would remain just a pipe-dream. Then I became interested in this murder case and was fascinated.

Having seen the date for which the trial was scheduled, I decided to go and observe. One thing led to another. I began taking notes and thought I could perhaps write a short article. I truly became hooked and, after writing so many notes, I realised I had the subject and the material for my book.

Writing this book felt like one of those 'Grand Designs' projects which are always much more difficult than you think, take twice as long and cost double your budget. If I had understood the huge commitment required, I would probably have never started. But I am glad I did.

Not realising how hard it would be and underestimating the work involved, it would simply have been impossible to complete without the support of the following people:

My wife Anthea who is easily the most selfless and hard-working person I know. For six months she took up the slack of all the chores I neglected to do and had to be satisfied with talking to the back of my head as I sat glued to my computer. Not only did she not complain or question my sanity, but actually encouraged me on the occasions when I was struggling. Thank you so much.

Stephanie, Alison and Michael are my (grown up) children. I am sure they all probably thought this was simply another of Dad's barmy projects (of which there have been many) that would probably come to nothing. If that's what you thought, thank you for not saying it out loud – at least not to me. You are all more talented than your father, so make the most of your talents.

During those long and sometimes tedious days spent sitting around the court complex, I would like to thank Matt and Sally for their help, kindness, patience and good company. When I discussed my project, you didn't sneer or roll your eyes (like some people did) you seemed genuinely interested and encouraged me in times of doubt. You'll never know how much that helped my confidence.

I have to give a mention to Roy who was probably more excited about my book than I was. You were always asking about the publishing date and were determined to be the first customer to buy my book. If you are reading this now, it must have actually happened.

Finally, to Helen at SilverWood. You held my hand throughout the publishing process and tolerated my naiveté with kindness and patience. Thank you for helping turn my pipe-dream into reality.